TO
  Pat
  who
  puzzles about our piety
  and
  sees beyond our skepticism
  and
  Maxine
  who
  takes us
  at
  face value

Christianity for Pious Skeptics

Christianity for Pious Skeptics

James B. Ashbrook
Paul W. Walaskay

Abingdon
Nashville

CHRISTIANITY FOR PIOUS SKEPTICS
Copyright © 1977 by Abingdon

All rights reserved.
No part of this book may be reproduced in any manner whatsoever without written permission of the publisher except brief quotations embodied in critical articles or reviews. For information address Abingdon, Nashville, Tennessee.

Library of Congress Cataloging in Publication Data
ASHBROOK, JAMES B 1925–
Christianity for pious skeptics.
1. Paul, Saint, Apostle. 2. Christian saints—Turkey—Tarsus—Biography 3. Tarsus, Turkey—Biography. 4. Bible. N.T.—Biography. 5. Faith and reason. 6. Christian life—1960– I. Walaskay, Paul W 1939– II. Title.
BS2506.A83   230   77-911
ISBN 0-687-07646-3

Text on page 99 is from "Little Gidding" by T. S. Eliot, from *Collected Poems 1909-1962*. Reprinted by permission of Harcourt Brace Jovanovich and Faber & Faber, Ltd.

Text on page 148 is from "Walking to a New Beat," composed and written by James Astman. Used with permission.

Scripture quotations unless otherwise noted are from the Revised Standard Version Common Bible, copyright © 1973.

Scripture quotations noted NEB are from The New English Bible. © the Delegates of the Oxford University Press and the Syndics of the Cambridge University Press 1961, 1970. Reprinted by permission.

Scripture quotations noted Phillips are from The New Testament in Modern English, copyright © J. B. Phillips 1958, 1960, 1972.

Scripture quotations noted JB are from The Jerusalem Bible, copyright © 1966 by Darton, Longman & Todd, Ltd. and Doubleday & Company, Inc. Used by permission of the publisher.

MANUFACTURED BY THE PARTHENON PRESS AT
NASHVILLE, TENNESSEE, UNITED STATES OF AMERICA

ACKNOWLEDGMENTS

We are indebted to Colgate Rochester Divinity School-Bexley Hall-Crozer in various ways. Both of us are graduates, although we attended in markedly different eras. We have been stimulated by the school's intellectual atmosphere and touched by its pietistic longings. Paul Walaskay served as chairperson of the Post-Easter Convocation in 1975. In that position he pressed for the theme of post-critical ministry. The committee selected James Ashbrook to deliver the Francis Wayland Ayer Lecture on the history and interpretation of Christianity, which he entitled "Arriving Where We Started: Beyond Critical Coolness and Uncritical Warmth." Earlier Walaskay presented a lecture series to a conference of American Baptist pastors in New York state on "St. Paul the Mystic: A New Model for Ministry."

We are deeply appreciative of the competent and patient typing of Nancy Root, Dana Gruttadaro Cone, and Ellen Bulmore of the divinity schools, who worked under the probing attentiveness of Joanne Oliver. We also appreciate Karen Materna and Paula Krawczuk of the University of Rochester, who, in addition to typing, managed our scheduling to discuss the issues herein contained. Finally, Linda Knoll of the House Church also is to be praised for her critical eye in catching mistakes in earlier drafts and for helpful stylistic suggestions.

Ashbrook's Ayer lecture appeared in *Foundations*, and his fourth chapter appeared in slightly adapted form in *Religion in Life*.

We are painfully aware of our limitations, yet very excited by the directions these ideas are taking us.

JBA and PWW
Lent, 1977

CONTENTS

PART I
The Mystic Experience of the Apostle Paul:
Recovery of a Model for Christian Living
Paul W. Walaskay

Introduction 15
I From Death to Life 19
II. Paul the Pharisee: Destruction of the Self 33
III. Paul the Christian: A New Creation 43
IV. Paul the Person: *Imitatio Christi* 60
V. Paul and the Church: One in Christ 77
Notes 82

PART II
Arriving Where We Started:
Beyond Liberal Criticism and Conservative Commitment
James B. Ashbrook

I. Dilemma and Direction: Two Brains and
Two Realms................................. 89
II. Using the Bible: Penetrating and Participating ..101
III. Speaking of God: Basis and Content 116
IV. Praying for the Spirit: Receptive and Active 127
V. Living for Christ: Limits and Affirmations 139
Notes 149

Epilogue: Wholeness of Soul and Oneness with God ...154

> I prefer to doubt rather than rashly define what is hidden.
> John of Salisbury, twelfth century

FOREWORD

From the earliest days of the Christian church, the relationship of revelation and reason has been the major problem confronting the faithful. To what extent is faith reasonable? To what extent is reason faithful? Should reason be abandoned to the demands of faith? Should faith be twisted to conform to the demands of reason?

Augustine started with revelation and proceeded to make reasonable judgments about the world. Aquinas claimed it was the other way around; one begins with reason that ultimately leads to faith. In the theologically turbulent twelfth century, John of Salisbury sought a middle path between the academic scholastics like Abelard and the cloistered mystics like Bernard. Luther was convinced that faith, when true to the demands of conscience, conformed with reason. Present-day fundamentalists insist that all conflicts between faith and reason must be resolved in the direction of faith. Liberals treat faith so flexibly that it continually bends to fit the contours of reason.

Like John of Salisbury we are "pious skeptics." Knowing the classical formulations of Christian faith, we attempt to live as committed believers; yet reason dictates that these formulas and our commitment be held accountable to human reason. On the other hand, it is abundantly clear that reason also has its limits; it can reach neither the ecstatic height of mystical experience nor the enfolding depth of human compassion.

CHRISTIANITY FOR PIOUS SKEPTICS

This book is for those committed to a life of faith yet open to the call of reason. We write for pious skeptics. We hope to direct the reader's attention not to new terrain, but perhaps to familiar landscapes seen in different ways. In the following pages we focus on that which constitutes the religious mind. Such a venture is presumptuous and slippery: presumptuous because we are aware of the limitations of probing the height and depth of religious experience and expression; slippery because "mind," after all, is a metaphor—to paraphrase the psalmist, "Who can know the human mind?" But these limitations notwithstanding, we take on the challenge of exploring the religious mind, what the apostle Paul calls "the mind of Christ." We are less interested in dissecting component parts and more interested in seeing the synthetic whole of religious expression and experience.

To help us see what is at once familiar yet obscure, we employ a hermeneutic tool—that is, a means of understanding and interpreting the recorded experiences of our forebears. This tool comes from the field of psychological research, which is nothing earthshaking in itself—writers ancient and modern have always been quick to apply their psychological insights to a given situation. What has contributed to our thinking, however, comes out of the literature known as the "psychology of consciousness." In a later chapter we cover some of the research that undergirds the thesis of this book.

For now let us simply state the conclusion that our single head actually holds within it two brains. Each half of the cerebral cortex performs distinctive work: the left hemisphere specializes in analytic, logical, verbal activity, while the right hemisphere functions as the area of holistic, integrative, perceptual, nonverbal cognition. We identify the left hemisphere, which controls the right side of the body, as the sphere of "intentional consciousness" and the right hemisphere, which controls the left side, as the sphere of "in-touch awareness."

In this book we apply the two brains to some of the dimensions of Christian life. We also suggest, after providing examples of the application of psychology of consciousness, that the religious mind strikes a balance between the two brain halves, thereby enabling us to live comfortably in the realm of reason *and* revelation as pious skeptics.

Western culture has been primarily "left hemispheric" in its application of rational thinking to almost every facet of human existence. One could cite endless examples in science, economics, politics, education, and even religion. Eastern culture, on the other hand, has been guided in the main by the right hemisphere with its nonrational view of life. There is no such thing as queuing up at a bus stop or a ticket office—one often feels fortunate that bus drivers bother taking the same route each time or that tickets are printed at all. Two brains have resulted in "split brains" and fractured faith.

Post-critical faith, the faith of the pious skeptic, is therefore a way of speaking about the religious person who has gone beyond the easy answers of simple (and often fundamentalist) faith and beyond the hard questions of complex (usually liberal) faith. The religious mind is one that ultimately transcends "critical coolness" (left hemisphere) and "uncritical warmth" (right hemisphere). Two brains—one mind—faith functioning fully!

Walaskay's opening essay responds to pious skepticism in a specific way. He steps firmly and deeply into the world of the apostle Paul and thereby into the world of the Bible. He brings to that exploration considerable biblical knowledge as well as broad contemporary insights. Crucial issues of biblical criticism are not neglected nor are they magnified out of proportion to the total picture of Paul as a person of faith, a model for post-critical faith. Theology takes on fresh vitality in recovering a biblical model for faith that holds ecstasy and ethics together as necessary to each other as the two sides of the divine-human encounter.

Ashbrook's essay deals with post-critical faith in a broader sense. He begins with the current research on the mind and thereby in the world of the scientific. He finds in the scientific a model with which to understand classical religious issues of the Bible, God, prayer, and Christ. Theology takes on a fresh focus in discovering an anatomical model for faith, one that holds receptivity and activity together as necessary to each other as the two hemispheres of the brain.

Walaskay's narrower base with broader focus and Ashbrook's broader base with narrower focus may, therefore, be regarded as a complementary unit. Ashbrook's essay begins where Walaskay's ends: the latter keeps faith clearly responsive to the God of the Bible as clarified in Jesus as the Christ; the former finds faith clearly related to what we are as human beings more particularly. Together these essays seek to acknowledge the thoughtful carefulness of criticism and to affirm the freeing commitment of faith. They endeavor to go beyond the seeming contradictions involved in believing what could supposedly be doubted.

Without elevating our efforts beyond the modest form that they take, we see ourselves as part of that persistent and prominent minority who, through the centuries, believes God is God of truth and worthy of trust. Faith without thought is blind; thought without faith is sterile. Truly, we would live beyond pious skepticism!

PART I
THE MYSTIC EXPERIENCE of the APOSTLE PAUL: RECOVERY of a MODEL for CHRISTIAN LIVING
Paul W. Walaskay
INTRODUCTION

In a recent article in the *New York Times Magazine* Andrew Greeley and William McCready asked the question: "Are we a nation of mystics?" Although they did not answer the question directly, they suggested that many more people have had mystical experiences than are publicly willing to admit. In fact, about 40 percent of fifteen hundred persons polled said that they had at one time or another experienced "a powerful spiritual force which seemed to lift them out of themselves." And "virtually all of the respondents have never spoken about their experiences to anyone"—especially, surprisingly and sadly, ministers. "One woman remarked that she could not mention it to her brother, who was one, because, as she said, the clergy simply don't believe in those things any more, and he would want her to see a psychiatrist."[1] Incredible! The fact that clergy suspect the mystics in their congregations to be covert schizophrenics probably means that one of the most important aspects of religious life is being written off by religious leaders as at least irrelevant and possibly psychopathic. It perhaps also means that people in the pews do not really trust the spiritual dimensions of their lives to their pastors.

This situation should be of concern to clergy and laity alike, not only because such a significant portion of the general population claim ecstatic experiences, but for a couple of other reasons. First, the intensity of the experience may well release tremendous amounts of non-neurotic creative energy that transforms not only the individual involved, but the institutions in which, and through which the individual works. We have long lived with the myth that the mystic has been a withdrawn, self-centered ascetic. Yet the great mystics of the Christian tradition show this to be patently untrue. From the apostle Paul through Augustine, Teresa of Avila, Catherine of Genoa, and Thomas Kelly, mysticism has gone hand in hand with mission; spiritual care for the self has led to physical care for others. Second, and more to the point of this book, the Christian faith has its roots in mysticism. We Christians owe our very incorporation into the body of Christ, the new Israel, largely as a result of Paul's mystical experiences beginning with his conversion and pervading the whole of his missionary career. It is with the first and foremost of Christian mystics that this work is concerned.

The objective of this part of *Christianity for Pious Skeptics* is to look at the life of Paul the apostle and to extrapolate from that survey some notions of what it is to be a Christian mystic living beyond the boundaries of belief. Like a three-pronged electrical plug, the biograhpical material of Paul's life is only the ground wire. By grounding this work in such an intense and significant person as Paul we are able to examine two current carriers of the Christian movement more freely: *eros* and *logos*, passion and reason, mystery and mission, ecstasy and ethics. Finally, we shall explore how "being in Christ" helped Paul integrate the two aspects—*eros* and *logos*—of the apostle's personality.

To help us understand the mind and spirit of Paul, I shall not only draw upon the standard tools of historical research—biblical criticism, comparative literature, linguistic analysis—but I shall incorporate some of the more recent developments from the field of psychology as well, specifically, the psychology of consciousness.

Even though historiography is a field-encompassing field, which makes use of contemporary psychological insights, I am well aware of the hazards and limitations of such an application. As long ago as 1913 Albert Schweitzer reviewed and critiqued the then current wave of psychiatric studies of Jesus—most of which concluded that Jesus was a schizophrenic, paranoid person. Schweitzer notes that the psychiatrists "busy themselves with the psychopathology of Jesus without becoming familiar with the study of the historical life of Jesus. They are completely uncritical not only in the choice but also in the use of sources."[2] More recently, church historian Roland Bainton has leveled the same criticism at Erik Erikson's psychoanalytic study *Young Man Luther*. According to Bainton, one who attempts to study the psychological features of a historical figure must not only be careful with the sources (one can get two quite different perspectives of a person depending whether one reads his enemies or his friends), but

> one must master the milieu of the subject of the biography. Nor does the milieu suffice. One must be familiar also with what preceded.... When all the material is amassed and critically sifted, lacunae appear. They can be bridged only by conjecture. The psychiatrist may well contribute to understanding by conjecture, but a surmise is not treated as a fact and used as the basis for another surmise. One who constructs a pyramid of conjectures may be compared to God who made the world out of nothing.[3]

So there are hazards along the way to be avoided. But one aspect of writing biography cannot be avoided and that is the psychological presupposition that any writer brings to his work. It is best, I think, to recognize and point out these presuppositions as they occur, and, in fact, consciously apply them when a piece of biographical data might be enhanced by such application.

I hope that we shall come to see Paul as he was—complex, conflicted, courageous. We shall see that he was not unlike us, sharing our passions, joys, sorrows, hopes, and visions. Perhaps as this portrait of Paul is unveiled we shall begin to identify new dimensions of ourselves—of our rich Christian heritage, of our wonderful possibilities for the present, and of our thoughtful and loving impact on the future.

I. From Death to Life

Most early spring days begin cool and sunny in southern Italy. This morning was no exception. Wild flowers sprayed the fields with yellow, violet, white, and pink. Squinting through the narrow slot to the paisley hillside across the valley he drew into his eyes the only color to invade this gray place. Everything turned gray here—walls, utensils, people—as if vital coloration was being drained in preparation for death. This rock-hewn cavern was the tomb's anteroom.

It had been two years since he and his lawyer arrived in Rome. Until now he had successfully appealed his case through the imperial court system. The charge against him fell into the catch-all category of *laesae maiestatis*, which was designed to eliminate a wide variety of political dissidents and troublemakers. Literally the term meant the "lessening of majesty"—anything that diminished the glory, authority, or power of the monarch. Such a sweeping charge was often difficult to prosecute and to defend; nevertheless, the charge was sufficiently serious in terms of national life and personal penalty that the evidence and testimony were treated with utmost care and consideration. The State could elect to act as prosecutor in the case. If the evidence seemed to indicate a serious threat to the imperial majesty, the State's own lawyers entered the case. If the State chose not to prosecute, the accusers could still press their case in the courts at their own expense.

The two-year statute of limitations had almost run its

course; in two weeks the prisoner would be released from house arrest. His accusers had not brought their case to Rome. He received friends; ate and drank with them; enjoyed their company and their stimulating, provoking conversation; swathed in their affection; and felt the calming glow of close friendship into the deep night. Friends for years, friends for life, there is no comparable wealth on earth; it is lavish and luxurious beyond material value because good friends conquer the original psychic disease of humanity—loneliness.

He patiently waited for his freedom, but freedom never came. It was with surprise and bewilderment that he took the news from his lawyer that the State had suddenly decided to enter the case against him. The prisoner would immediately be removed from his lawyer's home to a maximum-security cell in the great walled prison in the northeastern sector of the city. Before leaving the house he was stripped and reclothed with the loose, rough woolen prison tunic that served as a blanket for the cool spring nights and, for the unfortunate, as a burial shroud. So he was chained and led to the waiting cart that delivered him to the imposing prison.

After the brief admitting procedure in the warden's office he was led down a steep slope toward, he guessed, the rear of the prison. As he descended with his escorts into the pit of this strange world he noticed changes. Daylight was no longer directly visible; there were no windows, no skylights. The indirect light coming in through the small clusters of cells that they passed had to be supplemented with torches lining the narrow hallway. And the change in smell seemed to match the decreasing access to the freshness of the outside world. The new inmate felt himself already growing stale in this place. He observed one more thing along the way, something he naturally noticed because of his craft as a tent-maker. The structural materials of the fortress had changed. The upper level of the prison had roughhewn wood used for doorframes and ceiling beams; flagstone covered the floors; iron braces, hinges, and spikes were used here and there; and white, cracking lime covered the walls. At this level there was no evidence of man's craft—only stone, the natural stone foundation of this mountain fortress, surrounded the prisoner. There was no way of escape—no doors, no windows, and only a single entrance from a narrow corridor.

Suddenly the corridor flared to a large flat space with a semicircle of cells at the far end. In the open area there was one small wooden table and a stone stoop that served as a seat for the guard. As they reached the open area the guard rose, greeted his fellow guards, and took custody of the prisoner. The prisoner was amazed at the large number of cells arrayed before him; he did not count them, but there were seventy, each about six feet wide and eight feet deep with solid rock walls. It had taken a small army of slaves ten years to carve out this wing of the prison; it was an escape-proof design that had been simple and faultless, for none had escaped.

The prisoner was led to a stoop that jutted out from the wall in front of his cell. The manacles and chain were left connecting his hands and a shackle was bolted around his ankle. The long, heavy chain attached to the shackle was looped through a carved rock ring that extended outward from the wall between the cells like a massive teacup handle. The other end of the chain was connected to a prisoner's leg in the adjoining cell; there never was quite enough chain to move freely, which forced the prisoners to cooperate in their movements around the cell.

After the prisoner was hoisted by two guards through the small opening that stood about three feet above the stoop, he dropped through nine feet of darkness landing with a loud clank and a painful thud. His eyes slowly adjusted to the dim light. The torchlight performed a macabre dance on the wall far over his head. He quickly noticed one more source of light, a small pool of daylight coming in at the base of his cell. Where the floor met the outside wall there was a small carved slit, three inches high and about six inches long. Occasionally the slit was used to drain the floor of the cell; more often, it only served to let in small, unwelcome creatures (he soon learned to tear off part of his tunic and stuff it in the opening, but even that was ineffective—some rodents tolerated the taste of wool).

Before he could gather the courage to down his third breakfast of fetid prison gruel, a jarring yank on the long chain pulled him to his feet. The chain slackened then quickly tightened. He saw his foot, then leg, leave the ground; next his whole body was banging against the wall like a plumb-line weight. After he was hoisted to the opening and pulled through, he was informed by one of the guards that the Imperial Supreme Court was now prepared to hear his case.

The trial was surprisingly quick. The judge was appointed by the emperor to act in his name. A higher appeal was not possible, though a death sentence might be commuted by the emperor himself. The defendant was led into the courtroom, which was far smaller and more austere than he anticipated. There was nothing of the regal pomp and splendor that graced the provincial courtrooms where he had argued his case. He was disarmed by the very appearance of this ultimate room of judgment and its mute message of Spartan strength and curial efficiency. The office-sized room contained only six plain chairs, a small table for the court secretary, and a larger table for the judge. Once the lawyers were introduced to each other and to the judge by the secretary, the defendant was brought before the judge's table where he stood as the secretary slowly read the charge against him: "Inciting the populace to revolt against the imperial government and advocating allegiance to a rival emperor." The defendant's previously recorded disclaimer was also read to the judge. The accused had denied any involvement in riots in the Syrian province and the so-called rival emperor was in fact only a secular way of talking about the deceased founder of the defendant's religion. The judge asked the secretary if the defendant had been examined by torture in an attempt to extract a confession. The record indicated that he had been so tested by a beating, and his testimony remained unchanged. The judge then turned to the prosecuting attorney and asked him to present his case.

The prosecution produced two witnesses, a merchant in leather goods and a wine wholesaler. Both gave essentially the same terse testimony. They had heard the defendant plotting the destruction of Rome by fire with other conspirators. In his defense the defendant's lawyer suggested that the men did not overhear an arson conspiracy, but an apocalyptic discussion about the divine destruction of this world by fire—an innocent theological speculation. The judge questioned whether such "speculation" was too well timed with the great fire of Rome to be simply coincidental. Finally the prosecutor added a confession extracted from another suspect that named the defendant as the leader of the conspiracy. The defense was at a loss for an adequate explanation about the confession and weakly contested the legality of suddenly shifting the charge against the defendant from "inciting a riot" to "arson." The defendant was declared guilty of inciting a riot that led to the burning of the city. He was sentenced to death by the headsman's axe. Execution would take place within the week.

The prisoner was driven back to the fortress and dropped into his cell. Immediately his lawyer was at work preparing a brief to be submitted to the emperor whom he hoped would commute the sentence from execution to banishment. Three days before the scheduled execution the brief reached the emperor who barely scanned the thin volume, picking out a phrase or two where a word caught his eye. He could not have known that it was extremely well written, covering not only the two years of intricate legalities, but also including an incredible political apologetic—the defendant's outstanding record as a decent citizen, supporting attestations of political loyalty, and a summary of the defendant's political philosophy, which was conservative, bordering on old Roman republicanism. He was neither revolutionary nor reactionary. He believed strongly in the ideals of *pax Romana*—universal peace and harmony brought about by the Augustan reforms. Surely the emperor Nero, hailed by the Senate as the new Augustus, bringer of a golden age of peace and concord, would be generous enough to spare this political prisoner as he had spared hundreds before. *Clementia*, "clemency," had been a term most frequently used to describe his earlier reign, a quality one hoped would not be lost on this case.

The emperor turned to the political advisor who presented the brief and asked his recommendation. "No clemency" was the terse reply. The emperor merely nodded his concurrence and returned the brief. The imperial aide delivered the decision to the defendant's lawyer.

On the morning of the second day before the execution the lawyer was given permission to see his client. Again the condemned man was rudely jarred out of his sleepless stupor and hoisted to the area outside the cells. His lawyer looked haggard and drawn, his features—eyes, mouth, cheeks—were empty hollows, exaggerated by the dim light. Just one look at his advocate, and he knew the ultimate decision. As they sat together on the stoop outside his cell the two conversed about the trial, appeals, and verdict. The lawyer received instructions about the meager remains of the condemned man's estate. He also made a few helpful suggestions and agreed to transmit some personal messages to a couple of close friends.

They had lost, and losers celebrate strangely. The two asked for a piece of the cell keeper's stale bread. With a genuine sense of pity and sadness he gave them a generous portion. The defendant quickly broke off a piece of the loaf and returned it to the surprised jailer. Then the two shared what was left. They stood looking into each other's eyes until they had reached a silent sense of resolution, a mystical unity of spirit—then a warm and solid embrace, touching from cheek to toe, the last human warmth the prisoner would ever feel. There were tears and trembling and awkwardness as they slowly pulled apart. The jailer came over and quietly led the lawyer to the chief guard, who escorted him away. For the last time the prisoner was gently lowered into his cell as if gentleness was the last gift the jailer could impart to his condemned charge.

That night and the next day passed slowly. Wakeful fantasies merged with somnolent dreams. Childhood, adolescent, and adulthood experiences; opportunities seized, opportunities missed; pleasant times, occasional suffering; dear friends, close friends; intimate and ecstatic experiences; intimacy and ecstasy . . . and now, a tug on the chain from above disturbed his dreams, and he was aware of the soft morning light coming in through the drain-slot. Had the second night passed so quickly? He reached for the chain; this time he would be ready to hang on for the ride to the top. Once out of his cell his leg shackle was unbolted, and he was led up the long, narrow corridor. This time, however, they did not take the same route back to the main entrance; instead of going by the prison offices, they walked through a long galley of cells. At the far end was a large wooden door that the jailer unlocked and pushed open to the outside. The prisoner was led through the door, around the row of cells, and finally stopped at a semicircular terrace bordered by the prison in back and a steep cliff in front. Looking down into the deep valley and across to the flowering hill, the prisoner recognized that he stood directly above his cavern home of two weeks. Turning, he saw the "less dangerous" prisoners looking from their cell windows, curious about the impending execution. Their visual participation in this event was supposed to do more than satisfy morbid curiosity; it was meant to quench any smoldering desire to commit similar capital offenses.

The manacle was removed from the prisoner's left wrist and rebolted after his hands were forced behind his back. He gave a numb nod of recognition to his lawyer, who was allowed to collect his remains. A brief statement of the condemned man's crime and the judge's order of execution were read. The prisoner's knees buckled automatically as the huge axeman forced his head down onto the oak stump. His eyes were opened wide taking in the last view of life, the flowers on the hillside; his tongue was savoring the salt of his own sweat; his ears were alert, listening to every movement behind him. Suddenly there was a rushing, life-severing swoosh and explosion, instantly energizing every nerve and muscle in his body—arms smashing against their bonds, legs bulging with ultimate strength, veins and arteries outlining the arms and legs in a final attempt to store up life's blood. Then collapse, life gushing from the body. And from the mighty severed head, sight and taste and smell and finally sound dissipated into a senseless void.

I woke up startled, shaken by my subconscious that converses with reality. I hesitate to analyze this dream for you (though I have done it for myself). Perhaps it would be best simply to make two general observations. First, the dismemberment of the totality of our humanity—the severing of the head from the body, mind from feelings, reason from passion—is a continual threat. Occasionally the threat is carried out by friends, enemies, state, church, businesses, schools, and we feel trapped and powerless as the severing blow descends. There seems little we can do to hold together. Life collapses, our sense of self shatters under the blow. For most people this kind of blow is not ultimate—unlike the one in my dream. The fragments are reconstituted, passion is reunited with reason, *eros* is again linked with *logos*, the senses are revitalized. We come out of the depths, out of the senseless void. That which helps this process along—time is the cosmic healer—is beyond the scope of this book and better left explored by psychologists and philosophers.

The second observation is this: Although there are some interesting psychological nuances imbedded in the dream, it is my own imaginative reconstruction (and as a historian I know that there is precious little reliable data) of the apostle Paul's death. The dream reminds me that Paul was a flesh and blood human being. He would have been the first to denounce being reduced to stained-glass status. Unlike his master, that "rival emperor" Jesus of Nazareth, Paul had no Docetic controversies arise over him, no attempts to prove his sinless nature, no debates about his capacity to suffer, no nit-picking about the "Paul of history" and the "apostle of faith." Though he was a hero of the faith, he is not an object of faith; though he prayed to be released from suffering, his petitions were not granted; while others claimed for themselves a sinless existence, he simply claimed his own moral incertitudes and imperfections; while his converts quickly boasted of achieving a suprahuman spiritual existence, he reminded them of his own bodily weaknesses, limitations, and sufferings. He was simply a man, nothing more, as his enemies were quick to point out. Yet he was a great man, a man whose theology formed the cornerstone of Western civilization. And biographies of great men must take into account weaknesses as well as strengths, limitations along with lasting contributions, passion together with reason. The body and head are a living unit. The severing of the head from the body renders a person dead. Our objective, then, is to look at the "pre-execution" Paul, to reunite and restore that living being that Roman jurisprudence tried to destroy. And so we move from the end to the beginning, from dreamlike death to wide-awake life.

There are many ways to approach a study of Paul's life and thought. The history-of-religions school of the late nineteenth and early twentieth centuries attempted to present him in his cultural milieu.[1] It was out of this Greek-infested culture that Paul lifted several notions from the mystery religions (such as "dying and rising" with a god as an act of initiation into that deity's religion) and applied them to primitive Jewish-Christianity. Paul's genius was the welding of Greek and Jewish-Christian thought to produce a new religion palatable to the wider Hellenistic world.

There are those scholars who have narrowed their investigation to Paul's Jewish background. Paul, after all, was a rabbi, and a study of contemporary rabbinic teaching could reveal much about the apostle. Did Paul view Jesus as the "new Torah"? Did Paul come upon the notion of Christ as the last Adam by way of dialogue with his fellow rabbis? W. D. Davies and H. J. Schoeps have recently attempted to deal with these and other questions about Paul's relation to Judaism.[2]

There has been one recent attempt to understand Paul via Freudian psychology.[3] I shall return to this approach later because I think the field of psychology has given us some important tools for historical research, although Freud's seem quite blunt now.

Most biblical scholars, however, have bypassed a very practical consideration in their study of Paul: Paul was a minister of Christ, and more than that he remains the archetypal "minister" for all Christians—lay persons and professional clergy alike—who take seriously their Christian calling. Paul is the New Testament model of the minister. Yet Christians have continued to overlook the Pauline model of ministry, preferring to embrace the figure of Jesus as the "perfect minister," the "good shepherd," the "heavenly high priest."

The *imitatio Christi* has been more than a pious slogan for committed Christians; it has been the goal of a full Christian life. The difficulty of such a grand imitation, especially for those who maintain a "high" Christology, is that one cannot help falling short of full imitation. Can we struggling, imperfect humans even come close to the quality of ministry that we see in the Christ of the Gospels? The goal may well be unreachable and therefore constantly frustrating.

Because our natures are human, it may be easier to identify with the apostle Paul rather than Jesus as the, if not perfect, at least well-intentioned and compassionate minister. Paul, in all of his human frailties and weaknesses, was called by God to be a minister of Jesus Christ. Perhaps an *imitatio Pauli* is more appropriate for us who, in spite of weakness and frailty, attempt to be compassionate servants of Christ in the world.

But more than this—more than just another study of the life and message of Paul—prompts me to write. I want to reevaluate, and if possible restore, a dimension of Paul's ministry often ignored or overlooked by scholars and pastors alike—*the mystical dimension of existence.* The life of Paul, then, will be a vehicle by which we shall attempt to—

1. uncover the content and meaning of Paul's "Christ-mysticism" by using both historical and psychological tools;
2. render Christ-mysticism comprehensible to the contemporary reader by translating the Pauline experience into modern psychosocial thought forms;
3. reestablish the credibility—historical and psychological—of Paul's mysticism for the three following categories of contemporary persons:
   a. the large segment of churchgoers who do not claim for themselves a mystical (religious) experience—there was no "sawdust trail," no salvation experience, no flashing lights, no visions of Christ. I hope that this study will demythologize some of the unique claims made by the more "enlightened" brothers and sisters. Even though I want to establish the ecstatic ground of religious experience, I also want to show that such experience is not reserved for a chosen few; "being in Christ" is not the sole domain of the fundamentalist sects.
   b. the persons who highly value ecstasy as an important, perhaps *the* important, part of religious life. They will find ample support in the solid roots of this traditional Christian experience. But beware! This work stands as a warning not to indulge in the first deadly sin—pride. I want to reduce the lure of *hubris* by revealing the common base, universal availability, and widespread experience of being in Christ.
   c. and finally, the "closet mystics." I want to remind you that you are not alone; your experience is not so strange that it is not shared, it is not so obscure that it cannot be (at least partially) understood, and it is not without precedent. You are in good company.

I well remember that in my own seminary education four clergy models were presented in the course on the ministry. First was the priest, the combination museum curator/cultic officiant; second, the prophet proclaiming judgment and doom, setting the teeth of church trustees on edge as he parades with furrowed brow before the federal courthouse; third, the teacher who shares with his congregation the excitement of intellectual discovery; and finally, the pastor, always up on the latest therapeutic techniques—TA, Gestalt, tickle, primal scream, reality therapy—always waiting for the magic moment of transference.

In this study I want to have the apostle himself revive yet another often ignored dimension of Christian life—the believer as mystic. The above four models have to do with doing. For Paul, however, the other side of doing is being. The mystic experience is the experience of being that entails a recovery of the true, original self—a primordial self that reflects the state of humanity before the fall.

Before we embark on this study, a word is in order about sources. As with any study of Paul, our primary source of information is his own correspondence. After a hundred years of scrutinizing the style, vocabulary, theological content, grammar, and purpose of each letter in the Pauline corpus, a broad consensus has developed in the academic community with regard to the authenticity of the individual letters.[4] It is quite clear that Paul is the author of the Roman, Corinthian, Galatian, Philippian, and Thessalonian correspondence. The many detailed arguments pro and con on the authenticity of the remainder of the corpus are beyond the scope of this work. There is some doubt that Paul actually wrote Colossians and Ephesians, the former possibly the product of a Pauline secretary and the latter an encyclical cover letter for the collected Pauline corpus. There is considerably more doubt that Paul wrote the letters to Timothy and Titus. Yet the issue of authenticity need not detain us, for the autobiographical information contained in the "genuine" letters is sufficient for developing a portrait of the apostle.

Also, I have disregarded the biographical information in Acts for a variety of good reasons. First, it is biography, not *auto*biography, and it was written some forty years after Paul's letters. Second, the author of Acts does not even refer to, let alone use, Paul's correspondence. Third, with respect to the issue of Pauline mysticism, we shall see in later chapters how the Deutero-Pauline letters and Acts deviate from Paul's own concept of being in Christ.

It is our good fortune that there is so much autobiographical information imbedded in his letters. More than any of the other literary forms in the Bible, the letter conveys the stamp of the author's personality. The letter was a substitute for the face-to-face encounter and sometimes reflected the more profound personal concerns and emotional states of the author. All of Paul's letters reveal much of himself; his writings flow with the gamut of emotions. Philippians is characterized by a deep sense of thanksgiving and joy, while red-hot anger and gray anxiety abound in the Corinthian correspondence; Paul is perplexed and defensive when writing to the Galatians and respectful and controlled in addressing the Roman church. As Deissmann said so long ago, "Every letter of Paul is a picture of Paul, and therein lies the unique value of the letters as sources for a historical account of their author."[5]

I propose that we divide our study of Paul into four sections: Paul the Pharisee, Paul the Christian, Paul the person, and finally Paul and the church. Let us begin with the Pharisaic Paul.

II. Paul the Pharisee: Destruction of the Self

Paul of Tarsus was a Jew from his birth at about the beginning of the Christian era until his death in approximately A.D. 65. There is not a shred of evidence that he ever thought of himself as being anything other than Jewish. It is always with great pride that he speaks of his life as a Jew. In Philippians 3:4-5 he says, "If any other man thinks that he can be proud of his existence, I have reason for even more pride; I was circumcised on the eighth day [according to legal custom], born of the people of Israel, of the tribe of Benjamin [the tribe that remained loyal to the Davidic/Messianic dynasty], a Hebrew born of Hebrews [the ancient and honored title which Jews claimed throughout the empire]" (author's translation).

Paul was a Jew, but more than that, Paul was a Diaspora Jew—that is, a Jew of the Dispersion living in the world of Greek culture away from Palestine. It would be nice to know with certainty what life was like, especially for the Jewish community, in Tarsus of Asia Minor; that would give us considerable insight into the life and thought of Paul. What was he taught in school? How was his daily life at home and in the city? What did he see, what did he do? How did Jews relate to the wider Greek culture? What impact did the wider culture make on Judaism? To answer any of these questions would be exceedingly helpful in a study of Paul, but such direct information is scanty.

Though we cannot be certain what the impact of Judaism was on the Greeks of Tarsus and vice versa—primarily because we have no written records by or about the Jewish community in that city—this cannot (and will not) prevent us from making an educated guess about the cultural, philosophical, and religious exchange that must have made an impact on Paul—an impact confirmed in his writings. We *do* know that the Cilician port city, known as "the Athens of Asia Minor," was located in the heartland of high Hellenic culture. The worldwide traffic that flowed in and out of Tarsus brought, along with its goods, a steady stream of cultural peculiarities, philosophical points of view, and religious and mystery cults of all kinds. To be more specific, there is some evidence that Tarsus was the cultic center of the vegetation deity Sandan. As part of the mystery ritual, a figure of the god was burned on a funeral pyre (death by the withering summer heat) and rose to new life each year.[1]

We also know that Tarsus was a center of philosophical learning. The ancient geographer Strabo notes that "the zeal which the men of Tarsus show for philosophy and culture in general is so great that even Athens and Alexandria are surpassed." It was the philosophy of the Stoics (with which Paul shows acquaintance in his letters; especially Romans 1-2) that enjoyed great popularity under Athenodorous of Canana (*ca.* 74 B.C. to A.D. 7). To cite further direct information about Tarsus would not be greatly useful here, and we can only specualte that Paul may have seen the dying and rising ritual and that he was impressed by the Stoic scholars. But there are other indirect data that need to be taken into account and extrapolated onto the Jewish community of Tarsus.

First was the attempt by learned Jews of the Diaspora to come to terms with the wider culture—the production of the Septuagint (the Greek translation of the Hebrew Old Testament) and the philosophy of Philo are two well-known examples. One suspects that the Septuagint was translated not only for the Greek-speaking Jewish community, but for the heathen as well; the translation was, according to legend, commissioned by the chief librarian of Egypt to be added to the great books and read by scholars in the library of Alexandria. "Propaganda and mission to the Gentiles appear in the LXX [Septuagint] as a specific task incumbent on Jewish piety. . . . This universalistic 'pathos' of the world mission which was the very soul of Septuagint Jewish circles—and we must remember the many expressions in the LXX of referring to the whole, to 'all'—was alive in the young Saul of Tarsus, who chose as his vocation the mission to the Gentiles."[2] Furthermore, the Jewish philosopher Philo gave Diaspora Judaism one of the greatest boosts in the evangelizing process. He was not only conversant with the major strands of philosophy, but he was a supremely creative philosopher in his own right. He is most remembered for his allegorical method of biblical interpretation by which the stories of the Old Testament were set in contemporary parlance, given philosophical support, and provided Jew and Gentile alike with a common ethical foundation.

There are a few other pieces of evidence that Jews in the Diaspora attempted not only to accommodate to the Hellenistic culture, but also tried to win converts to their way of life.[3] Certainly the Jews of the Diaspora could not go on year after year feeling the burden of guilt that their life outside Palestine was God's continuing judgment; their "exile" had more purpose than divine retribution for the sins of their fathers. The prophet Isaiah had foreseen their role in history as "a light to the nations"; many in the Diaspora took Isaiah seriously and lived in the Hellenic world with a genuine sense of mission. The Jewish historian Josephus and the book of Acts are our best supporting sources of such a mission. In his work *Against Apion*, Josephus mentions not only that Greeks are continuing to convert to Judaism, but that Greek philosophers and the masses have been impressed with Jewish custom to the point of imitation. In the *Jewish War*, Josephus suggests that the Greeks of Antioch were attracted to the synagogue services in great numbers. The Acts of the Apostles supports this statement of Josephus, for in Acts 13:16 Paul addresses the "God-fearers" who are present in the synagogue at Antioch. The crowning achievement of Jewish missionary activity is proudly recorded by Josephus who describes at length the conversion of the royal house of Adiabene.[4] The second-century Christian apologist Justin Martyr accurately reflects the notion that Judaism regarded itself as teacher of the Gentile world. Finally, we remember the saying of Jesus that the Pharisees traversed land and sea in search of one convert (see Matthew 23:15). Such was the zeal that Judaism had in its missionary program outside of Palestine.

Members of the Hellenistic synagogues seem to have been quite liberal toward their Gentile neighbors; they were satisfied if the "God-fearers" drawn from the heathen into the Jewish community simply pledged themselves to confess belief in the one God and to observe a minimum of ritual and ethical commandments. No demands were made for circumcision—not all were required to become proselytes, full members of the Jewish people.

The leaders of Palestinian Judaism appear to have disapproved of this laxity with respect to the law, insisting upon circumcision for all (in Acts 15 even Christian leaders in Jerusalem struggle with this issue). Nevertheless, in the mission field outside of Palestine the liberal heart ruled.

Perhaps the Diaspora "liberality" was only exchanging favor for favor, for Judaism had long been recognized as a legitimate religion and was looked upon with toleration and respect.[5] Jews were free of work obligations on the Sabbath, they were allowed to pay the yearly half-shekel temple tax that supported the cult in Jerusalem, they were exempted from serving in the military, and they were not required to sacrifice to the emperor—though they promised to pray *for* him. These privileges may have made their Greek neighbors jealous—sporadic clashes are recorded—but they also may have enticed pagans to look more closely at Judaism as a possible way of life.

On balance, I believe that relations between Jews and Greeks were peaceful and, more than this, that Jews made a conscientious effort to be at peace with their neighbors and win them over to Judaism if possible. Let us now return to Paul.

It is the obvious thing to say that Paul, in his childhood and youth, was influenced by Hellenistic Judaism as practiced in the synagogues of the Diaspora. By his experience in the synagogue and the home his character was probably marked with the spirit of toleration toward his non-Jewish neighbors—as much out of defense as a minority as from real missionary concern. This concern was reinforced in the synagogue by learning the rudiments of reading and writing with the Bible as a textbook. And his Bible was the Septuagint, for whenever he quotes the Old Testament it is from the Greek text. Paul was what Adolf Deissmann called a "Septuagint Jew." Not only his prose but his piety as well is from the Greek scriptures with their implicit concern for the Gentile world. It has often been suggested that Paul is responsible for a fusion between Hellenism and Judaism that produced Gentile Christianity; one should remember, however, that such a fusion had been underway for three centuries before Paul.

Furthermore, we can surmise that Paul took full advantage of the education offered him. He did indeed surpass his colleagues. He not only developed the rudimentary literary skills, but learned his philosophical, exegetical, and rhetorical lessons well. We have already noted that Paul was acquainted with the Stoic notion of discovering

God and God's will through creation (Romans 1–2); he was also familiar with such Stoic concepts as conscience, freedom, reason, virtue, endurance, sobriety, and duty. Like Philo, he occasionally used the allegorical method of biblical interpretation (*e.g.*, the Sarah and Hagar allegory of Galatians 4), and he had mastered the rhetorical form used by itinerant preachers and philosophers of the time, the so-called diatribe that advanced philosophic, moral, or religious ideas without long-winded deductions, speculative arguments, and technical language. Often in his letters Paul's diatribe takes the form of a lively debate, outlining an imaginary opponent's objections and making the reader a partner in the discussion.

The young man Paul no doubt had well ingrained in him not only a serious and well-educated attitude toward his religion, but also a very liberal attitude toward human beings who stood outside the law and a deep sense of concern that somehow they too might be included in the people of God.[6]

Eventually Paul, the brilliant undergraduate in Asia Minor, felt the call of God to pursue his theological education and enrolled at the best of the rabbinic schools studying with the best of the rabbinic scholars in Jerusalem, Gamaliel the Elder. In Philippians Paul says proudly that he attached himself to the Pharisees, the most strictly orthodox school of thought both in manner of life and in mission. As noted above, the brand of Judaism that Paul discovered in Palestine would have been somewhat different from his experience of Diaspora Judaism. Pharisaic Judaism in Palestine had a tendency from the time of the reconstuction and reformation under Ezra and Nehemiah to insist upon racial and ritual purity. Conformity to Torah would insure the continuing existence of Israel as the people of God. This hardening and particularizing of theology did not really let up until the destruction of the temple in A.D. 70

when Jews were forced to abandon the cultic center and reestablish their identity in the synagogues of the Diaspora.

It was as a rabbinic student in Jerusalem that Paul advanced in Judaism beyond his contemporaries, so extremely zealous was he for the traditions of his fathers, the oral and written Torah (see Galatians 1:13-14). Paul probably possessed the zeal of a convert from the lax and insufficient religion of his parents to the rigorous and demanding life of the rabbinic scholar. It is entirely possible that Paul took a more severe and rigid view of Pharisaic Judaism than his masters would ever have intended. In his zeal for his newly found Pharisaic faith he attempted to destroy the newly organized sect of Judaism; in doing so he was in effect destroying the liberal tendencies that were already etched deeply in his being. Paul the conservative Pharisaic Jew had turned against Paul the liberal Hellenistic Jew, so that in attempting to destroy the church—liberal Hellenistic Judaism in the extreme—he was destroying part of himself.

We know that from Paul's own words his persecution campaign was only against the Hellenistic Christian communities outside of Palestine. Paul notes that he "was still not known by sight in the churches of Christ in Judea", for they had only heard secondhand that "he who once persecuted us is now preaching the faith he once tried to destroy" (Galatians 1:22-23).

On the surface, Paul's statement that he was not known by the Judean (including Jerusalem) churches flies in the face of the Acts accounts of persecution. Acts 8:1-3 states that on the day of Stephen's martyrdom

> a great persecution arose against the church of Jerusalem; and they were all scattered throughout the region of Judea and Samaria, except the apostles. . . . But Saul [Paul] was ravaging the church and entering house after house, he dragged off men and women and committed them to prison.

The relationship between the persecution of the Jerusalem church and Saul seems clear. Again in Acts 9:13 Paul was charged with doing evil to the "saints *at Jerusalem.*" In 9:21 the question is raised, "Is not this the man who made havoc *in Jerusalem* of those who called on this [Jesus'] name?" Finally, in Acts 26:10 Paul says, "I did so in Jerusalem [opposed the 'name of Jesus']; I not only shut up many of the saints in prison, by authority from the chief priests, but when they were put to death I cast my vote against them."

Yet there is another series of passages in Acts that suggests that Paul's persecution was outside Judea as he indicates in Galatians 1:21-23. In Acts 9:2; 22:5; 26:11-12, the author of Acts mentions that Paul's persecution was aimed at the Christian community of Damascus in Syria. This clearly agrees with Paul's own statement that after his conversion and sojourn in Arabia he "returned to Damascus." This return, I would suggest, is after his original trip from Jerusalem to Damascus for the purpose of persecution.

On balance, I trust Paul over Acts on this detail. Paul may have brought Christians from the Diaspora to Jerusalem for trial, he may have received orders from the Jerusalem high priest to travel to Damascus for the purpose of destroying the aberrant sect, but he probably did not directly attack the Jerusalem church. Had he been such a persecutor, "breathing threats and murder," he certainly would have been recognized by sight upon his return as a Christian.[7]

At best, Luke the historian is hedging on the relationship between Paul and Jerusalem. In all of the passages that suggest this relationship one could infer that Paul's "havoc" is dragging Diaspora Christians into Jerusalem for trial and imprisonment. At worst, Luke the historian is simply inaccurate.

But there is other evidence that the Jewish-Christian community of Jerusalem would not have impassioned Paul to persecution. We can surmise on fairly sure grounds that Palestinian Christianity was more like Pharisaic Judaism than was Christianity in the Diaspora. There is ample evidence that the Christian church in Judea had close ties with the Pharisaic party. Acts 15:5 relates that "some believers belonged to the party of the Pharisees." Paul indicates in Galatians 2 that James, the brother of Jesus and head of the Jerusalem church, argued for the church to maintain circumcision and a kosher table. Finally, Josephus, a Jewish historian and contemporary of Luke, claimed that those who were "strict in observance of the law" (*i.e.*, the Pharisaic party) were offended by the execution of James, the brother of Jesus, at the hands of the Sadducees.[8]

Paul could not have been interested in persecuting the Jewish Christians of Palestine; they had remained relatively loyal to the Torah, and he could not fault them for venerating a crucified messiah. Belief in Jesus as the Messiah was neither blasphemous nor a sufficient reason for persecution. It just made Christians appear to be an odd and deluded sect of Judaism. Any Jew could keep such folly as long as he attempted to live within the limits of the Torah.

From the beginning of his life to the very end Paul remained a Jew. Even in his classic Christian letter to the Romans Paul can say in the form of a prayer:

> I am speaking the truth in Christ, I am not lying; my conscience bears me witness in the Holy Spirit, that I have great sorrow and unceasing anguish in my heart. For I could wish that I myself were accursed and cut off from Christ for the sake of my brethren, my kinsmen by race. They are Israelites, and to them belong the sonship, the glory, the convenants, the giving of the law, the worship, and the promises; to them belong the patriarchs, and of their race, according to the flesh, is the Christ. God who is over all be blessed for ever. Amen. (Romans 9:1-5)

But Paul's Judaism had undergone a significant change. As a youngster he had been raised as a liberal Hellenistic Jew. In Jerusalem he converted with the fervor of a zealot to Pharisaic Judaism and turned against his former self, becoming rigid and dogmatic in his insistence that the Hellenistic Jewish Christians, who were not very dissimilar from the God-fearers of his home synagogue in Tarsus, be obliged to conform to the Pharisaic pattern of religious life that he learned in seminary in Jerusalem. But this inward trouncing of the spirit could not last; Paul was ready for yet another transformation.

III. Paul the Christian: A New Creation

There have been a variety of ways of understanding Paul's conversion, and the common thread through all of them is the notion that his conversion was the resolution of an internal conflict. Some scholars have alluded to Romans 7, describing Paul as caught between the demands of the superego and the id, that the struggle lay between his desire to comply fully with God's law and an interior compulsion that inhibited his obedience. Other scholars have presented more exotic and interesting explanations of the apostle's conversion claiming for him an epileptic fit, an hysterical outbreak, or the resolution of his sexual identity. Still others reject any possibility of a psychological explanation, seeing rather the workings of divine grace, which can turn the worst enemy of Christ into a faithful servant. Richard Rubenstein has rightly said that "no attempt at explanation can do more than offer a very partial illumination of what took place."[1] Nevertheless, Paul's conversion was a key event in the life of the apostle, and indeed in the life of the whole of Western culture. We must keep pressing to discover what happened to Paul in the midst of his pogrom of the Hellenistic Christian community.

In his classic work, *The Varieties of Religious Experience*, William James has noted that conversion experiences fall into two broad categories.[2] The first is the volitional conversion experience in which there is a gradual building up, piece by piece, of a new set of moral and spiritual habits. Those who experience volitional conversion sense within them an awakening to an appreciation of religion; it is a subconsciously maturing process, an opening of the heart to what the mind already knows. The second category of conversion is the self-surrender type. It is in this category of conversion that William James places Paul. The person who experiences this kind of conversion most typically says, "I will not give up; but when my will was broken, it was all over," or "Man's extremity is God's opportunity." There are two things in the mind of the candidate for self-surrender conversion: first, the experience of present incompleteness or wrongness or "sin"; second, a positive ideal that the potential convert longs to incorporate into his own life. When the act of yielding to a larger power finally takes place, "a complete division is established in the twinkling of an eye between the old life and the new."[3] Augustine most readily comes to mind as an example of the person who had undergone this kind of conversion. Augustine, you will recall, was the delightful half-pagan/half-Christian who chased women by night and by day would pray, "Lord make me chaste, but not yet." For him Christianity was an either/or proposition: either chasing women or being chaste. Perhaps it is because we are conditioned by the conversion model of Augustine that we have come to put Paul in this same category.

But one must ask, Does Paul really belong here? Paul both radically rejects the old—"Whatever gain I had in Judaism I counted as a loss"—and claims the past, even boasting of his life in Judaism—"If anyone thinks he has confidence in the flesh, I have more, . . . righteous and blameless under the law." Paul's conversion, then, cannot be thought of as that of a penitent sinner rejecting his recent past; rather Paul has put the rabbinic tradition in the service of his personal experience. Nor can we see in Paul's conversion the resolution of a struggle between two competing systems of thought—Hellenic and Judaic. As we have already noted, Hellenistic Judaism was a synthetic movement some two centuries old. Paul's conversion experience seems not to fit either of James' categories. What then was Paul's experience of conversion? What did the revelation of Christ mean to him?

Three colorful descriptions of Paul's conversion are presented in the Acts of the Apostles (9:1-19; 22:4-16; 26:9-18). Though it is very tempting to use these stories for our study of Paul's mystic experience—heavenly lights, voices, and visions—we must forego this luxury. The significant differences between the three accounts raise questions about Luke's accuracy in recording the tradition; furthermore, the contradictions between the Lucan presentation and Paul's own understanding of his conversion and call are insuperable.

Let us examine the differences among the three stories in Acts: (1) in 9:7 Paul's companions remained standing, in 26:14 they all fell to the ground; (2) in 9:4 and 22:7 Paul fell to the ground while his companions remained standing, in 26:14 they all fell to the ground; (3) in 9:6-19 and 22:10-16 Paul was told by Jesus to go to Damascus where he received instructions from Ananias to be a witness, in 26:16-18 Paul was commissioned by Jesus at the time of the vision to be his witness and apostle. The differences between the first and second point are relatively unimportant if we allow Luke the literary latitude any historian of antiquity deserves; we should remember that Luke wrote his account fifty-five to sixty-five years after the conversion event, and much can color oral and written tradition over that period of time. But when one compares the details of the third, especially the first two accounts, with Paul's own account of his conversion in Galatians 1:13-17, we run into serious problems.

In the Galatians passage Paul expressly states that he did not receive his apostleship from men nor through a man, "but through a revelation of Jesus Christ." Kirsopp Lake lays out the contradiction between the first two Acts accounts and Paul:

> By no possibility can these [Galatian] statements be reconciled with the story that Paul did not receive his commission directly from Jesus. . . . If Paul had wished to contradict the story in Acts, could he have selected a better phrase than that which he employs when he says he is an apostle "neither from men nor through a man"?[4]

Moreover, there is another detail of Acts that does not square with Galatians; that is Paul's stay in Damascus after his conversion. In Galatians, Paul says that he did not immediately go to Jerusalem (it took him three years to get there), but instead went to Arabia then returned to Damascus. In Acts, on the other hand, Paul spent a few days in Damascus and then went straight to Jerusalem. Again Lake is pointed, and I could not express his conclusion better.

> All these discrepancies raise the same problem. They are of that simple and direct nature that admits of no compromise. Either we take Paul's version, or that of Acts. Paul was a principal in the story, and he was writing nearer the events. There can be no doubt that in general his version ought to be followed. The question remains, how far does this affect our confidence in Acts? It seems to me absurd to say that Acts does not suffer. When a witness has been put in the box and proves to be slightly wrong on almost every point, and very wrong on some, his evidence on other questions is to be treated with caution. Nevertheless those who have had most to do with witnesses are the most reluctant to define the exact limits which this caution ought to be given. Few ever give quite accurate testimony. Luke was collecting information; he heard other stories besides Paul's. If he got them confused, and sometimes did not follow Paul's own account, it is not surprising.[5]

Lake also notes that Luke probably had before him a Jerusalem tradition about Paul that, like his enemies of Galatians 1–2, tried to claim that his apostleship was conferred by men, the leaders of the Jerusalem church.

We cannot, therefore, rely on Acts as a source of information about Paul's conversion, but this will be, I believe, to our benefit. We are on safer ground when we resist the temptation of using Acts and restrict ourselves to Paul's own words. Paul says very little in his letters and never dwells on the details of his experience. There are only two passages (I Corinthians 15:8 and Galatians 1:15-16) where Paul speaks of the revelation of Christ to him; neither of these portray the experience as a "conversion" of the Damascus road type, but rather point to the birth (and not even "rebirth") of the apostle. In I Corinthians 15:8 the Revised Standard Version weakly translates Paul's statement, "last of all, as to *one untimely born*, he appeared also to me." Most modern translations, being a bit bolder, translate *ektromati* as "abortion, monstrous birth." Though Paul's metaphor is interesting, it is not very understandable. What does it mean to say that Christ had appeared to an aborted fetus? Such a revelation has no chance of survival. A few commentators have suggested that Paul is reflecting the slanderous epithet hurled at him by his enemies—Paul was the monster-come-lately to the Christian movement. But there are two other possibilities. First, *ektromati* may simply mean an unexpected birth, a surprising event. Paul's apostleship is a surprise to everyone, including himself. Second, Paul may not be using *ektromati* as a metaphor but as an indication of how Paul really understands the revelation of Christ to him. "Lastly," says Paul, "as to one not yet due to be born (*e.g.*, a fetus), Christ also appeared to me." It is, therefore, not impossible, and in fact probable, that Paul has come to realize that while he was yet a fetus, Christ came to him.

47

This may well be the case especially when one considers the second passage, Galatians 1:15-16. Paul says, "He who had set me apart *before I was born,* and called me through his grace, was pleased to reveal his Son to me." Like Jeremiah before him, Paul had been called while yet in the womb to be not a prophet, but an apostle of Jesus Christ to the nations. Jesus had been with him from birth; he had been revealed to Paul *in utero*. Though the Damascus road story in Acts is vivid and colorful, the decisive event of Jesus coming into the apostle's life occurs not as an adult, but as an unborn child. Election and revelation had come to Paul in the womb. Paul's conversion means that he was put in touch with his primordial being. The revelation of Jesus is at the same time a revelation of the deepest self.[6]

How is it, then, that Paul as an adult came to recognize what had been with him since birth—the call and revelation of Jesus Christ? In all probability the spirit of Christ was awakened in him through the very opponents he persecuted; like all oppressors he learned something about himself from his enemies. So Paul the oppressor was conquered by the oppressed. The warmth, the mutual care, the joy expressed by these Hellenistic Christian communities could not have helped reawakening within him his deep and long-lost affection for the Hellenistic synagogue. Through the body of Christ, the church, he was able to transcend the limitations of the law and recover his own spirit.

Perhaps I can illustrate my understanding of Paul's conversion, which seems to fit neither of William James' categories, by telling you of the experience that I have shared with many theologians my age. My early religious upbringing took place in a warm, joyful, and simple fundamentalist church. Our church friends were affectionate and generous with one another as they were with outsiders who occasionally came to our services. When I went off to seminary that old narrow, literalistic, and unbending theology was replaced by the intellectual delights of Bultmann and Tillich. I remember feeling, as did many of my contemporaries, how wrong the folks back home had been.

In *Leaves from the Notebook of a Tamed Cynic*, Reinhold Niebuhr tells of a letter (which many of us could have written) that he received from a young pastor.

> He was suffering for truth's sake. He had been merely telling his congregation that Jesus was a great spiritual teacher, as was Confucius or Laotsze, and that the Christ idea was the product of Greek legend and ancient mythology. His good people were so ignorant, he thought, that they failed to show proper appreciation of his learning and resented his iconoclasm.
>
> I find myself reacting violently to the sophomoric cocksureness of this young fellow. . . . For the life of me I can no more reduce Jesus to the status of a mere Galilean dreamer and teacher than I can accept the orthodox Christologies. The person who can make no distinction between a necessary symbolism and mythology seems to me no better than the wooden-headed conservative who insists that every bit of religious symbolism and poetry must be accepted literally and metaphysically. . . . Some of the supposedly ignorant peasants against whom my youthful friend is drawing his heroic sword may have more truth on their side than any fresh young theologue could possibly realize.[7]

So it was with Paul as with many of us—while I gained my intellect I lost my soul. But I suppose like good wine we mellow with age. The more exposure I have to the wine cellar of the world—contact with the rare vintages as well as this year's bottlings—the more my rantings and ravings against the "enemy" cease. Do I dare call it the spirit of Christ that now unites intellect and soul, sensitivity and skepticism, *eros* and *logos*, love and reason?[8]

Salvation for Paul was wholeness. In the middle years of his life the spirit of Jesus finally emerged as the integrating force that bound together Paul's tremendous sense of tradition (which the rabbis knew as written and oral law) with his deeper experience of humanitarian liberality and warmth. Unlike Augustine, Paul discovered that life could not be put into either-or categories. For Paul it could not be either law or experience; life is both-and. For Paul, Jesus had united law and liberty, tradition and experience.

As a result of his conversion, Paul became more than an advocate of the Hellenistic Christian churches; he also felt the call to create these communities himself out of the Hellenistic synagogues. He went to the Jew first and then to the Gentile.

Paul's mission was to help push away at the already liberal tendency of Hellenistic Judaism, opening more widely the doors of the synagogue to the Gentile. When the synagogue failed to respond, Paul would simply cross the street and start a house church composed of Gentiles, "God-fearers," and Jews who allied themselves with Paul. For Paul, Christianity was the true Judaism, taken just one liberal step further than that of the Diaspora synagogue.

Once Paul had realized that his contact with Jesus had been a primordial experience, leaping back in his own history past his years as a Pharisaic Jew, past his years as a Hellenistic Jew, to the very time when he was conceived, Christ became a very real and increasingly vital experience. There can be no question that Paul felt an intimate oneness with Christ, but what was the content of "being in Christ"? The so-called Christ-mysticism of Paul has been the subject of much theological debate and discussion over the last fifty years. When one thinks of Paul's Christ-mysticism, several passages come to mind. In Galatians 2:20 Paul writes, "I have been crucified with Christ; it is no longer I who live, but Christ who lives in me." Again, in Philippians 1:21 he writes, "For to me to live is Christ, and to die is gain." These are only two of the more familiar passages in which Paul claims union with Christ. That Paul uses the formula "in Christ" at least fifty times only underscores the fact that this was an important aspect of his Christian experience.

Any study of the mystical experience is loaded with difficulties. At first glance such a study would seem to be a contradiction in terms. How can one study with any degree of confidence an experience that comes to such a small portion of the human population? Moreover, that small population is spread throughout all cultures and all ages, from the trickle of aboriginal shamans to the contemporary flood of yogis, gurus, and monks. Not only is the small mystic population culturally and temporally diverse, the raw data of the experience are at best difficult to collect. The vocabulary of the mystic is highly colored, ambiguous, and metaphorical; more often than not the utterings of mystics are downright vague. How is one able to describe an "ineffable" experience, as Greeley and McCready so nicely put it, "to fathom the unfathomable, explain the inexplicable, eff the ineffable"?[9] So often when I press members of our local ashrams to describe for me the content of their mystical experiences the typical formulation that comes stumbling out is: "Like, wow . . . it's just an incredible inner peace, oh man, it's an experience, fantastic, wow!" With his eyes set in a "thousand yard stare" directed at my receding hairline, he leaves me to wonder about the meaning of "wow," "incredible," and "experience." While I too—as all people do—have occasional experiences of awe, mystery, and inner peace, I still wonder if there is more meat to be found on the bones of silence, nonsense syllables, the flight of the soul to the "alone," and the embrace of the interior being—all of which seem to resist any systematic and schematic reduction. While it may be impossible to say just what the mystic experience is and how one attains it (the transcendental meditation people are in a sense right; it is tailored to the individual), we can make some broad generalizations about Christian mysticism.

First, we ought to distinguish between two types of mystical experience in the Christian tradition: Christocentric and theocentric mysticism. As the terms suggest, the goal of one is unity with Christ, the goal of the other is unity with God. Paul is the first and foremost Christ-mystic; it is his experience of being in Christ that sets him apart from his Hellenistic mystical contemporaries and Christian followers who were seeking ways of "being in God." The mystical goal of Augustine, for example, was to be in God: "Our hearts are restless until they find rest in Thee." In a less popular but equally illuminating passage Augustine says: "I love a certain kind of light and sound and fragrance and food and embrace in loving my God, who is the light and sound and fragrance and food and embracement of my inner man."

Evelyn Underhill, in her classic work on Christian mysticism, claims that psychologically the transcendent (theocentric) and incarnate (Christocentric) mystics form

> the complementary reactions of two different types of mind to the grace of God. . . . The greatest and most truly characteristic of the Christian mystics, from St. Paul onwards . . . embrace in their span both those aspects of man's fullest and deepest communion with Creative Love.[10]

A second generalization about the nature of Christian mysticism has to do with intuitive knowledge and perceptions of reality. From the days of Aristotle to the nuclear age, the flow of human knowledge has been directed by "the scientific method." That phrase crystallizes and epitomizes the rational approach to the world. First one impartially observes natural phenomena, then the data are collected, next relationships between the data are drawn, and finally working hypotheses are formulated that help us better understand and predict the workings of nature. In going through this process over and over again, we have built up an immense data bank that scientifically describes the "real" world—our sensible world. The mystic, however, would contend that we must qualify that description. The Neoplatonists, for example, would assert that scientists have merely given an imperfect description of an imperfect copy of reality. (Scientists have recently affirmed the first part of that statement—all descriptions are to some degree imperfect. Not only are all things in a constant state of flux, but the very participation of the observer can alter the relationship.) The Christian mystic would claim that the real world is the world of interiority, the trip through inner space in search of union with God. To be so concerned with describing the natural world is of dubious value and drains off energy needed to pursue the spiritual life. Materialism (undue concern with the world of matter) is a snare, and purgation of earthly concerns is the first step in the spiritual pilgrimage.[11] Augustine said, "My life will be *real* life when it is full of Thee." That "real life" is reached not by cognition, but by intuition. Mystics reach not outward to measure and weigh, but inward to absorb and pray. Mystics are the artists of religion, "able to see and hear created beauty to which average eyes and ears are closed."[12] They impart to us a vision of reality that goes beyond what we know in our everyday life.

Third, we know that there seems to be a relationship between union with divinity (whether transcendent or incarnate), intuitive knowledge that leads to a reality beyond the world of linearity and causality, and how one approaches the sensible world of objects. Most of us view this world in a rather piecemeal fashion. As I sit writing this sentence in a forest above Cayuga Lake, I see a tree next to our fireplace, another tree by the car, then several other individual trees scattered around our cabin and down the steep bank to the lake. I begin with the particular (a tree) and move toward the universal. If I now close my eyes I can form a generalized image of, as my three-year-old daughter so aptly says, "treeness." I move from existential reality to essential reality. The mystic seems to have a head start on us because he begins with a view of life that is essential and universal. Such Christian concepts as grace, mercy, and love are not entities concocted by dogmatic theologians and mechanically applied to select individuals or even to all humankind; they are rather attributes of divinity experienced especially by the two great New Testament mystics, John and Paul, who perceived their universal significance. God's grace, mercy, and love pervade the cosmos. The mystic then moves easily from union with these divine attributes to the most universal of all categories—divinity itself. Over forty years ago Albert Schweitzer wrote that "recognizing the unity of all things in God, in Being as such, the mystic passes beyond the unquiet influx of becoming and disintegration into the peace of timeless being, and is conscious of itself as being in God, and in every moment eternal."[13] Being knows no time; in the fullness of eternity, being intersects worldly time so that at the mystic moment *all* of the past is summed up and crystallized, and there is a nucleus in that crystal that is pregnant with all the possibilities for the future. To be one with God is to be one with the "all."

Our mention of time and eternity leads to a final consideration already mentioned in this book—the primordial nature of the mystical experience. Mircea Eliade notes that recovery of a pre-Fall, paradisiac state has been the experience of mystics in almost every culture. "The mystical experience of primitives is equivalent to a *journey back to the origins*, a regression into the mythical time of the Paradise lost." By means of his mystical experience the shaman's ecstasy is able to restore the beatific state of humanity before the Fall. "It renews the friendship with the animals; by his *flight* or ascension, the shaman reconnects Earth with Heaven; up there, in Heaven, he once more meets the God of Heaven face to face and speaks directly to him, as man sometimes did *in illo tempore.*"[14]

Carl Jung points us in a direction that "Christianizes" this aspect of mysticism. In the passage that follows one cannot help but think of Paul. Christ, claims Jung,

> is the still living myth of our culture. He is the culture hero, who, regardless of his historical existence, embodies the myth of the divine Primordial Man, the mystic Adam. It is he who occupies the center of the Christian *mandala*, who is the Lord of the Tetramorph, *i.e.*, the four symbols of the evangelists, which are like the four columns of his throne. *He is in us and we in him.*[15]

The Christian mystic, then, is the person who is able to intuit a reality beyond the sensible world. That reality is composed of universal categories by which the mystic understands life. In contemplation and prayer the mystic seeks ultimately to be unified with the supreme universal category of reality, transcendent, or incarnate divinity.

In 1931 Albert Schweitzer's *Mysticism of Paul the Apostle* appeared in the British and American book markets. It was an ambitious attempt not only to deal with Paul's mysticism, but to review and evaluate the varieties of interpretation about the great apostle and his mystical experience. With the ease of a master swordsman, Schweitzer's pen quickly dispatched Reitzenstein (Pauline mysticism was dependent on the Hellenistic mystery religions), Bousset (Paul *and* the primitive church borrowed from the mystery religions), and Deissmann (Paul's Christ-mysticism is rooted in Jewish-Hellenistic thought forms).[16]

According to Schweitzer, Paul was an original and creative theologian who developed the notion of Christ-mysticism neither from an observation of Hellenistic mystery religions nor from a Philonic Jewish-Hellenistic mystique, but from his own experience of the Christian sacraments. "Without baptism there is no being in Christ! The peculiarity of the Pauline mysticism is precisely that being-in-Christ is not a subjective experience brought about by a special effort of faith on the part of the believer, but something which happens in him as in others, at baptism."[17]

Schweitzer has convincingly shown Reitzenstein to be wrong: Paul's mysticism was not derived from the Hellenistic mysteries. Nevertheless, it has also been suggested, and I think the suggestion is true, that Schweitzer's understanding of Pauline mysticism is overly mechanistic. In an earlier work, *Paul and His Interpreters*, Schweitzer bluntly stated that at the moment of baptism "the dying and rising again with Christ takes place [in the believer] without any co-operation of will or thought on his part."[18]

The problem, however, with both Reitzenstein's and Schweitzer's views of Paul's Christ-mysticism is that both result in a dissolution of Paul's personality. If Paul were a Hellenistic mystic, then he would have lost himself in union with God, in absorption into the divine world; Paul would leave off his humanity and become a god. Paul never speaks of "being in God." To be in Christ does not mean for Paul a loss of self, a loss of ego. Even in the most esoteric of Paul's statements in II Corinthians 12:1, he can boast about being *a man* in Christ caught up to the third heaven hearing divine secrets that cannot be repeated. In his mystical experiences Paul does not lose track of himself; he is still *a man* in Christ, a self-identifiable person having an ecstatic experience.

Nor does Schweitzer do justice to the apostle's personal experience of Christ when he reduces being in Christ to being part of "the body of Christ."[19] Granted that corporate identity was important throughout Israelite and Jewish history, does Paul really lose his personal identity to the community? Again we can point to that very same passage from Second Corinthians, which suggests that Paul's experience in Christ is a very personal experience not related to his being in the church; in fact he cannot even relate things he has personally heard to those who are in the church. Moreover, a corporate mystical experience of the intensity Paul describes for himself is highly unlikely. We have no evidence from his letters that suggests a shared ecstatic experience of being caught up into Paradise.

Rather than a loss of personal identity to either the divine world or the earthly corporate community, I see Paul's experience of Christ as one of coming in touch with his deep, essential self. Perhaps Paul took seriously the Delphic oracle: "Know thyself." For Paul the revelation of Christ brought the apostle to a revelation of his innermost being. The revelation of Christ meant salvation, wholeness for Paul, the integration of education and experience. The Messiah of the Christians had been in Paul since birth, calling him not to be Paul the Hellenistic Jew nor Paul the Pharisaic Jew, not even to be Paul the Christian, but simply to be the primal Paul—a new creation open to all the possibilities of life unhindered by the precedence of prejudice of the past, the plan or program of the present.

In commenting on Romans 12:2 ("Be transformed by the renewal of your mind"), Carl Jung has similarly suggested that *"Christ exemplifies the archetype of the self."*

> Despite the word *metamorphousthe* ("be transformed") in the Greek text of the above quotation, the "renewal" (*anakainosis, reformatio*) of the mind is not meant as an actual alteration of consciousness, but rather as the restoration of an original condition, an *apocatastasis*. This is in exact agreement with the empirical findings of psychology, that there is an everpresent *archetype of wholeness which may easily disappear from the purview of consciousness or may never be perceived at all until a consciousness illuminated by conversion recognizes it in the figure of Christ.*[20]

Paul in Christ was a new creature, a new being, a primal man ready as an adult to fulfill his divine calling.

Christ-mysticism was Paul's unique contribution to the church. More than his debates about the effectiveness of the law (which reflect the trend toward antinomianism already begun in the Hellenistic Christian communities), more than his struggles with the ethical consequence of freedom in Christ (which Paul often resolves in the direction of contemporary Stoic ethics), Paul universalized his personal experience of being in Christ to envelop the church, the human race, the cosmos. He saw that the universal was contained in the particular. As we shall see in the next section, at the heart of the mystic experience is a profound sense of personal *unity*. Unlike most mystics, however, Paul was not content to claim this unity in Christ for himself.

The church is one, experiencing a mystical unity in Christ. Paul's use of the term "one" is instructive for us. The church is a community baptized into *one body*. The people of the Corinthian church have missed the mystical significance of the Lord's supper. "If you're hungry, eat at home!" says the apostle. "It is by one spirit, unity in Christ, that we eat one loaf of bread, the one body of Christ, the mystical nourishment of the Church, and drink from one cup of wine, the life-blood of Christ, the spirit of the Church" (see I Corinthians 17-34).

All are one in Christ: "For as many of you as were baptized into Christ have put on Christ. There is neither Jew nor Greek, there is neither slave nor free, there is neither male nor female; for you are all one in Christ Jesus" (Galatians 3:27-28).[21]

Just as the experience of Christ brought Paul back to his primordial existence where he recovered his essential being, so the church in its experience of Christ has become the primal community, the new creation. In the old creation there was racial (Jew/Greek) strife, class (slave/free) struggle, and sexual (male/female) discrimination. In the new creation all are one in Christ, a unity that does not destroy the distinctions that make humanity interesting (the gnostic goal was that all, male and female, should be one—male!), but rather gives to all an equal share of dignity, respect, and responsibility in the life of the Church.

The mystic experience of Christ means for the Church a recovery of the primal essence of humanity, the new creation. The Paulinist who wrote Ephesians captured Paul's universal application of his personal experience rather well. God has elected us, the church in Christ,

> before the foundation of the world, that we should be holy and blameless before him. He destined us in love to be his [children] through Jesus Christ, according to the purpose of his will, to the praise of his glorious grace which he freely bestowed on us in the Beloved. In him we have redemption through his blood, for the forgiveness of our trespasses, according to the riches of his grace, which he lavished upon us. For he has made known to us in all wisdom and insight the mystery of his will, according to his purpose which he set forth in Christ as a plan for the fulness of time, *to unite all things in him*, things in heaven and things on earth. (Ephesians 1:4-10)

IV. Paul the Person: Imitatio Christi

So far we have noted that as a bright young man from the Hellenistic city of Tarsus, Paul traveled to Jerusalem to find his vocation as a rabbinic scholar. Discovering the strength of his intellect he sought to quell the "weaker" side of his humanity, that generous and tolerant side that had been nourished by the spirit of Hellenism. For the young rabbi it was law over freedom, tradition over experience, and he manifested the zeal of a convert to Pharisaic Judaism in his pogrom against the Hellenistic Christian churches. In the experience of persecuting the enemy he was also destroying part of himself, the part that was liberal, humanitarian, and tolerant—the spirit of freedom. In the face of the enemy Paul came to see who he really was. The Christ who came to him drew him back in time through his experience as a Pharisaic Jew, back through his youth as a Hellenistic Jew, back in time to his primordial beginning, back to his essential self, back to the experience of being "I." The call of God and the revelation of Christ had been his *in utero*. His statement in I Corinthians 15:10 is very illuminating: "By the grace of God I am what I am." Though Paul may be all things to all men, the revelation of Jesus given to him by the grace of God reveals to Paul who he really is—"I am what I am."

Perhaps it is coincidental, perhaps it is only looking for support two thousand years after the fact, but the research results reported by Greeley and McCready in the *New York Times* article on mysticism noted in the Introduction correspond largely to my own understanding of Paul, the first Christian mystic. One could construct a profile of the "typical American mystic." (It feels so strange even to write such a phrase. Americans? Mystical?) He (yes, men are more likely to be mystics than women) would be—

1. middle class (earning more than ten thousand dollars per year);
2. more likely to come from a "high church" (Episcopalian) than a fundamentalist sect;
3. black (those whites who claimed mystical experiences were not inclined to be racially prejudiced).

The mystics that Greeley and McCready contacted tended to be well-educated, well-integrated, contributing members of society. The energy released by their intense mystical experiences found expression in creative and nonpsychopathic endeavors. They described their childhood as being happy, where religion was a joyous experience (the father was more outwardly joyful in his religion than the mother). As Greeley and McCready point out, it is not likely that contemporary American mystics are running from something—either horrid backgrounds or unsavory present circumstances.

The parallels with the apostle Paul are striking. As a tradesman (tent-maker) and Roman citizen, Paul obviously fits into the empire's middle class. His conventional political rhetoric in Romans 13:1-7 attests to his high valuation of citizen responsibility to the imperial government.[1] Remember also that Paul was Jewish, a distinct racial minority in the Roman empire, and one could hardly be more educated or "higher church" (synagogue) than to be a "Pharisee of the Pharisees" who studied with Gamaliel the Elder in Jerusalem. If the religion of his childhood was as joyous in the Diaspora synagogue as I suspect it was, this provides yet another correlation (though we are getting dangerously close to a circular argument/proof here). One final item that deserves mention is the great reluctance of most people to share with others any knowledge (let alone details) of their experience. It was an experience that most people had once, would not care to repeat again, nor are they disposed to talk about it with anyone, especially the clergy. When Paul speaks of his charismatic (certainly mystical) experience he says: "I thank God that I speak in tongues more than you all; nevertheless, in church I would rather speak five words with my mind, in order to teach others, than ten thousand words in a tongue" (I Corinthians 14:18-19). Second Corinthians 12:1-10 shows how very difficult it is for Paul to describe his divine ecstasies; even to speak of them makes him feel like a fool.

In 1972 Richard Rubenstein published *My Brother Paul,* laying heavy emphasis on the psyche of the apostle that is clearly dependent upon analytic psychology. The conflict in Paul lay between the demands of the law, which Rubenstein translates as "the ego's common sense realism," and the human drive for immortality, which for Rubenstein is "the id's refusal to recognize any limitation of space, time, or mortality." This conflict was resolved by Paul's messianism; for Paul, Christ had "overcome mankind's terminal affliction"—death. "In messianism the abolition of the reality principle is projected into the future."[2] Jesus had become Paul's "older brother"; Jesus, according to Paul, is "the first-born of many brothers." Jesus as the older brother not only leads the way for Paul to immortality (if Jesus can rise from the dead, so then shall Paul someday), but as the older brother, Jesus also mediates between the father and his children.[3] Jesus' resurrection from the dead means that Paul may radically reject "the ultimacy of all pre-messianic institutions. Paul now rejected more than the law: he rejected worldly status, worldly power, and worldly wisdom, for he saw them as manifestations of the world of death and dying."[4] Paul does not reject the law because it is burdensome, but because it is superfluous in the messianic age. Christ is the end of the law and the beginning of freedom—the triumph of id over ego.

As interesting as Rubenstein is in his application of Freud to Paul, it seems stiff and overly determined by Rubenstein's own experience in psychoanalysis. We certainly need not limit ourselves to Freudian structures in probing the Pauline personality; there has been much shifting and squirming on the analyst's couch over the past fifty years. Exciting new approaches are open to us in our search to understand the depth and breadth of the human intellect and emotion, increasingly helpful ways to comprehend such a complex historical figure as the apostle Paul.

Now I am quite sure that many of my colleagues in New Testament studies will be appalled by what is to follow; they will conclude (perhaps rightly) that I am overpsychologizing in my approach to the apostle Paul. Yet, it is simply impossible to try to understand the theology, Christology, soteriology, and eschatology of Paul without making some assumptions about his psychology. It would be more helpful, I think, to realize that psychological assumptions are always being made, to recognize with some clarity what those assumptions are, and to use them where appropriate.[5]

My own interest in the Pauline personality was triggered when reading Second Corinthians I stumbled across this statement of Paul in 5:13: "If we are insane (*exestemen*), it is for God; if we are sane (*sophronoumen*), it is for you" (author's translation). Reinhold Niebuhr once quipped, "It is almost impossible to be sane and a Christian at the same time."[6] I suppose that all of us contain mixed measures of sanity and insanity, of madness and reason. This passage from Second Corinthians enticed me to look further at all of the places where Paul uses the language of madness and reason; I discovered that Paul's sanity language clusters around two sections of his Corinthian correspondence: I Corinthians 1–4 and II Corinthians 11–12.

In the First Corinthians passage Paul says that

> Christ did not send me to baptize but to preach the gospel, and not with rational wisdom (*sophia logou*), lest the cross of Christ be emptied. For the word of cross is folly (*moria*) to those who are perishing, but to us who are being saved it is the power of God. . . . But the Jews demand signs and the Greeks seek wisdom, yet we proclaim Christ crucified, a scandal to the Jews and foolishness to the Gentiles, but to those who are called, both Jews and Greeks, Christ is the power of God and the wisdom of God. (I Corinthians 1:17-24, author's translation)

Paul proceeds to be more specific about how his own teachings came across to the Corinthians.

> When I came to you, brothers, I did not come proclaiming to you the testimony of God with sophisticated arguments or wisdom. Rather I decided to know nothing among you except Jesus Christ and him crucified. For I was with you in much weakness, fear, and trembling; and my speech and my message were not persuasive words of wisdom, but the demonstration of spirit and power, that your faith might not rest in wisdom of men but in the power of God. (I Corinthians 2:1-5, author's translation)

Paul goes on to insinuate that though he could have imparted wisdom to the Corinthians they were not mature enough to receive it; they were not yet spiritual people, but people of the flesh, babes in Christ. He finishes his lengthy diatribe still on the defensive: "If anyone among you thinks that he is wise in this age, let him become a fool that he may become wise. . . . We are fools for Christ's sake, but you are wise in Christ" (I Corinthians 3:18; 4:10).

In the midst of this lengthy section on the foolishness of God and the wisdom of men, Paul relates his own insecurity and inability to communicate the gospel effectively. At least some in the church in Corinth simply shake their heads and dismiss him as a raving idiot.

In the Second Corinthians passage Paul also links foolishness with his own difficulty in speaking the gospel. This time Paul is defending not his message but his apostleship.

> I wish you would bear with me in a little foolishness (*aphrosunes*). Do bear with me! . . . I think that I am not in the least inferior to these superlative apostles. Even if I am unskilled (*idiotes*) in speaking, I am not in knowledge (*gnosis*). . . . I repeat, let no one think me foolish; but even if you do, accept me as a fool (*aphrona*), so that I too may boast a little. (II Corinthians 11:1-16)

Paul again feels on the defensive and forced to brag about himself.

> Are they Hebrews? So am I. Are they Israelites? So am I. Are they descendents of Abraham? So am I. Are they servants of Christ? I am a better one—I am talking like a mad man (*paraphronon*). . . . I must boast; there is nothing to be gained by it, but I will go on to visions and revelations of the Lord. . . . And to keep me from being too elated by the abundance of revelations, a thorn was given me in the flesh, a messenger of Satan, to harass me, to keep from being too elated. Three times I besought the Lord about this, that it should leave me; but he said to me, 'My grace is sufficient for you, for my power is made perfect in weakness.' I will all the more gladly boast of my weaknesses, that the power of Christ may rest upon me. For the sake of Christ, then, I am content with weaknesses, insults, hardships, persecutions, and calamities; for when I am weak (*astheno*), then I am strong (*dunatos*). I have been a fool! You have forced me to it. (II Corinthians 11:22–12:11)

Once again Paul relates the trouble he has in speaking to the problem of being perceived as a fool; yet, on the other hand, Paul sees things more than others, he has revelations and visions in abundance, and that for him is the ultimate sanity, a thing to boast about. Abundance of visions and lack of speech, sanity and insanity, weakness and strength, are significant contrasts in the Pauline personality. In Second Corinthians he says, "I am sane for you, but crazy for God": I am rational among men, but divinity brings about my irrationality. When I am weak, then I am strong. There is strength in weakness, and weakness in strength.

There are two sides to Paul's being: strength/weakness, sanity/insanity, speech/vision, foolishness/wisdom. There are of course other contrasts as well in the life of the apostle: he was tender and severe, humble and proud, joyful and depressed, in motherly travail over the Galatians and fatherly in his encourgement toward the Thessalonians; he was a mystic yet well grounded in this world; he was a man whose humble scratchings of pen on parchment, whose troubled correspondence to troubled churches has become sacred scripture; a man whom not a single contemporary historian mentions and yet who became the cornerstone of Western civilization.

The recent literature about the psychology of consciousness has led me to some surprising insights about Paul's complex personality. The term "consciousness" is a vague concept that refers to the integration of all types and modes of awareness within an individual. It involves such aspects as an inward awareness of sensibility (a system of internal perception), an awareness of self, and an awareness of unity (the fusion of internal and external stimuli). This implies that emotion and thought, intuition and cognition, are so integrated that the mind works as one entity. Our complex brains are able to sort out, compartmentalize, and relate often very diverse pieces of information. Just think about all the transactions the brain must make when we drive a car; auditory, perceptual, sensual, logical, spatial, and temporal calculations are constantly in play.

In his book *The Psychology of Consciousness*, Robert Ornstein suggests that there are two major modes of consciousness within the brain: the verbal-logical and the nonverbal-intuitive. On the basis of experiments performed with split-brain people (those who through accident or surgery have had the right hemisphere of the cerebral cortex severed from the left, a severing of the inner connecting fibers called the *corpus callosum*), we know that the left side of the body is controlled by the right side of the cortex and the right side of the body by the left side of the cortex. We also know that in the normal person the two hemispheres tend to specialize—the left hemisphere specializes for analysis, while the right hemisphere seems specialized for holistic mentation.[7]

> The left hemisphere (connected to the right side of the body) is predominantly involved with analytic, logical thinking, especially in verbal and mathematical functions. Its mode of operation is primarily linear . . . [and it] seems to process information sequentially.
>
> [The right hemisphere, on the other hand,] is primarily responsible for our orientation in space, artistic endeavor, crafts, body image, recognition of faces. It processes information more diffusely than does the left hemisphere, and its responsibilities demand a ready integration of many inputs at once. If the left hemisphere can be termed predominantly analytic and sequential in its operation, then the right hemisphere is more holistic and relational, and more simultaneous in its mode of operation.[8]

There is a right- and left-hemispheric duality in human consciousness, a duality long ago recognized in other cultures; the Chinese yin-yang symbol neatly displays the duality and complementarity of the two modes of consciousness. These modes have been called

female—male
light—dark
spatial—verbal

nonrational—rational
receptive—active
acausal—causal
yin—yang

All of these belong to the left and the right hemisphere respectively.

Most of us live our lives as left-hemisphere people. My calendar is linearly ordered by the half hour so that the day's program is often neither exciting nor stimulating, but predictable; I walk from building to building on campus over a rather narrowly defined map of pathways; my lectures normally contain a logical sequence of information, one piece of data adding upon another until a conclusion is reached.

While most people do live this way (and I am thinking primarily of my own context in the academic community), others exhibit a reliance on the right hemisphere. Aside from the obvious examples of musicians, poets, and painters, there are many who are highly intuitive. I think that children, for example, unhampered by left-hemispheric education, have such an innate intuitive understanding of the world about them. A short while ago my three-year-old daughter was talking about her experience at her sitter's house where she goes each day. She was telling me of a little girl there who does nothing but sit in a chair all day long. She just sits by the hour and, no matter how much she is coaxed, will not budge off the chair to play with the others. When I asked Rachel what the problem might be, she answered, "I guess Caroline is afraid inside." Astounded by such mature insight I continued to press my daughter (one should remain content with small victories). When I asked Rachel what she might do about the situation she exclaimed, "I could hit her!" Not only did she have an intuitive and accurate understanding of what was going on inside Caroline, she also intuited an effective (and not inappropriate) remedy.[9]

Robert Ornstein terms the shift in consciousness from the individual, piecemeal approach to knowledge to a more receptive, holistic mode, the "mystic experience." There are three characteristics of this experience: First is a consciousness of unity, or oneness. A second characteristic is the sense of realness—a reality that transcends the world of linearity and causality. And finally the contents of the mystic experience are often said to be ineffable, incapable of being fully communicated by words or by reference to similar experiences in ordinary life.

Ornstein also suggests that the way to make the shift from left- to right-hemispheric experiences is by upsetting, destroying, the normal lineal construction of consciousness. This may be accomplished by meditation, fasting, ritual dance, and certain psychoactive drugs. "A result of this 'turning off' of the input selection systems seems to be that, when the same sensory input is later introduced, we see it differently, 'anew.'"[10] The process is similar to taking a vacation ("turning off") from the routine way of dealing with our world. When we return, the familiar surroundings and tasks appear fresh, new, and different; our awareness has become "deautomatized." The "I" informs the eye; a new "I" sees a new environment.

Though we cannot be certain at all how it is that Paul was able to move from one mode of consciousness to another, from the left hemisphere to the right, we do know that he could claim the mystic experience. In that experience Paul discovered an internal unity. In I Corinthians 15:10 he says, "By the grace of God I am what I am." The experience of Christ in him, Paul's Christ-mysticism, put him in touch with his primordial being, his essence, his self. The revelation of Christ had come to him in his mother's womb. For Paul, Christ was the power of God, the *dunamis* of being (see I Corinthians 1:24). And Paul meant that term "being" not only in general ontological terms, but specifically with reference to himself: "Christ in me, the power of God in me, the *dunamis* of my being." Paul experienced the power of being by the grace of God:

> "My grace is sufficient for you, for my power is made perfect in weakness *(he gar dunamis en astheneia teleitai)*." I will all the more gladly boast of my weaknesses [the weaker side, the right-hemispheric experiences], that the power of Christ may rest upon me. . . . For when I am weak, then I am strong. (II Corinthians 12:9-10)

Thus we see perfection, wholeness in weakness, effected by Christ the power of God. Paul experienced an internal unity. He was more than a Pharisaic Jew, more than a Hellenistic Jew; from his conception he had been in Christ, and as an adult he realized that being in Christ meant having the power of God, the power of being itself. No more clearly was this power self-evident to Paul than in his weaknesses—in his inability to verbalize (weak left hemisphere) and his many visions (strong right hemisphere): "I have seen things that are not utterable." The ineffable vision is the mark of the Christ-mystic. In his quest for sanity he had become insane for God.

The Chilean psychiatrist Claudio Naranjo suggests that
> the relationship between the quests for sanity and enlightenment might be seen as that between the minor and the major mysteries of antiquity. While the former aims at the restoration of *"true man," "original man,"* the goal of the latter was the transcendence of the human condition, the acquisition of some degree of freedom from the needs or laws that determine ordinary human life by assimilation to a radically *different state of being.*[11]

Naranjo's description of the mystic fits Paul rather well. Paul's mysticism is a quest for both sanity *and* enlightenment; he recovers for himself the original, primal, true man, and he enters a radically new state of being, the new creation.

A similar result has been achieved for many by years of intensive psychotherapy—the weekly stripping away of excess baggage to lay bare one's true self and suddenly discover a new world, a new creation. Let me use just one illustration, again from Naranjo, of such an experience accelerated by drug therapy.

In *The Healing Journey*, Naranjo presents the case study of an engineer in a management job who was also a professor of business administration who had come for psychotherapy. He felt insecure, pressured, and vulnerable. His goals for therapy were "to know where to go in view of what I have. I want to be better, useful, and achieve new happiness. In the most intimate part of myself I have always been unsatisfied. I want to be sure of my work. This is my greatest problem, which prevents me from deciding and takes away the direction from my life." After two months of weekly appointments he agreed with his therapist to take a drug called methylenedioxy amphetamine, MDA. What happened with the drug was a trip in time back through his adulthood filled with anxiety and a search for God, back to his very earliest experience of love, not with his mother but with his wet nurse—"a really womanly woman." He came to see that during childhood his parents had managed to make him betray his love for this ignorant peasant so that he might love them the more, though deep down he had always loved her and had lived in gratitude for her. At the end of his trip the patient relates,

> Somewhat with my mother, later [I loved her], but not the same. And this, which was so strictly mine, I forgot and postponed. This is the root of the sorrow: having abdicated from myself. I found it: *the sorrow of having abdicated from myself!* I won't take it any longer. I am going to be what I am and whatever I may be![12]

Paul can say, "By the grace of God, I am what I am, I will be what I can be." For Paul, it is Christ who gives unity to his existence. Paul is strong and weak, sane and insane, foolish and wise, and it is his mystical experience of the risen Christ that allows him to live this bimodal existence without anxiety. And the unity Paul experienced in Christ extended in two directions: inward to his innermost, primal self and outward to the whole of the cosmos.

There is one final but important bimodal aspect to Paul's Christ-mysticism that I want to explore: ecstasy and ethics.

I mentioned at the outset of this book that an *imitatio Christi* may well be a pious concept far beyond the grasp of most modern-day Christians. I also suggested that perhaps an *imitatio Pauli* may be more within our grasp. Paul himself is well aware of the full demand and weight of *imitatio Christi*, for he twice admonishes the Corinthians to be "imitators of me, as I am of Christ" (I Corinthians 4:16; 11:1). Doesn't this negate the Pauline notion that all should experience direct contact with the risen Lord? Why would Paul put himself in the way?

The Corinthians were not yet ready for the full impact of Christ-mysticism; they were not yet spiritual persons, but "babes in Christ" (I Corinthians 3:1). This leads us to a final question about the nature of Christ-mysticism as understood by Paul. On one hand the experience of being in Christ was a truly esoteric, ecstatic, revelatory experience. This aspect of Christ-mysticism the Corinthian Christians knew well. They were making bold claims about their many spiritual gifts—tongues, prophecy, healing—all magnificent, all praiseworthy, all useful. Paul may well have had these Christians in mind when he said: "If I speak in the tongues of men and of angels, . . . if I have prophetic powers, and understand all mysteries and all knowledge, . . . but have not love, I am nothing" (I Corinthians 13:1-2). Anyone who settles for the mere trappings of mysticism is at best a "babe in Christ." For Paul that which completes the mystic experience is love, *agape*. To possess both the ecstatic experience and agapeic love renders the person "in Christ" mature. By "love" Paul does not mean an expression of sentimental fraternity (*philea*) or romance (*eros*), but a rational willing of the good for the neighbor (*agape*). This means that the mature Christ-mystic takes ethics (left hemisphere) as seriously as ecstasy (right hemisphere). It is significant that Paul begins his long section (I Corinthians 11–14) on spiritual gifts with a word about ethics in the church: "When you gather together, it cannot be the Lord's supper you are eating. For in eating, one of you greedily devours his own meal while another is left starving, and yet another is drunk" (I Corinthians 11:20-21, author's translation).

Ecstasy and ethics, mystery and mission, *eros* and *logos*, *charis* and *agape*—all of these dualities pervade the writings of Paul. They derive out of his being in Christ and they point to a still deeper dimension of being in Christ. Consider again Paul's willingness to serve as a mediator between Christ and the Corinthian Christians: "Be imitators of me, as I am of Christ." It was clear to Paul that they were not ready to be imitators of Christ. They knew ecstasy, but they were learning ethics. It is only when the two become united that they could become imitators of Christ, for only then would they be ready to share in his passion. Paul knew very well that the Corinthians were far from this stage of readiness; therefore he would protect and guide them (indeed, chastise them if need be) as a father (see I Corinthians 4:14-16).

Ecstasy *and* ethics become the mark of the full Christ-mystic that leads to a sharing of the suffering of Christ.

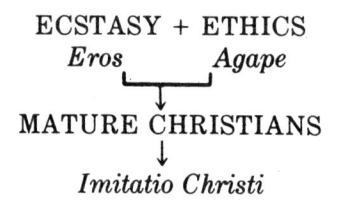

$$\begin{array}{c} \text{ECSTASY} + \text{ETHICS} \\ \underbrace{\textit{Eros} \qquad \textit{Agape}} \\ \downarrow \\ \text{MATURE CHRISTIANS} \\ \downarrow \\ \textit{Imitatio Christi} \end{array}$$

Though there are passages in Philippians (1:20-23; 3:8-11) and First Corinthians (4:10-16) in which ecstasy and ethics ultimately lead to "a sharing of his passion," perhaps the best example we can cite, and an appropriate passage on which to close this study of Pauline mysticism, comes from Paul's letter to the Colossians.

I have avoided using Colossians as a primary source in this study of Paul because of the continuing uncertainty about its authenticity. It is true that in Colossians there are many significant words not found in Paul's other letters (complete being of God, angel worship, new moon, severity to the body, etc.), but many of these may have been called out by the situation that the Colossian church faced; Paul may have reflected the language of those who were challenging the faith. It is also true that the Greek style of Colossians is loose and ragged—more so than Paul's other letters. Participles are strung together yielding lengthy, complicated sentences, a translator's nightmare. Yet, this could have been due to the haste and tension under which Paul worked to get this letter to the harassed Colossian Christians. Finally, there are some theological elements in Colossians that differ from Paul's other letters. The person and work ("reconciliation") of Jesus are seen in much more cosmic dimensions (see Colossians 1:15-17, 20-22; 2:15). Paul's use of the body metaphor in describing the church undergoes a change in Colossians; in I Corinthians 12:12 we are all parts of the body of Christ, the church, but in Colossians 1:18 the church is described as "the body" while Jesus is its "head." But even these theological differences cannot prove that Paul was not the author of Colossians. One hopes that the apostle's thinking was able to evolve and that he did not feel hidebound to repeat what he had written in his earlier letters.[13]

It is on the issue of mysticism that the authenticity of this letter can be decided in favor of Pauline authorship. Consider this significant passage, Colossians 1:24-29:

> Now I rejoice in *my sufferings* for your sake and in my flesh *I complete what is lacking in Christ's afflictions* for the sake of his body, that is, the church, of which I became a minister according to the divine office which was given to me for you, to make the word of God fully known, *the mystery hidden for ages and generations but now revealed to his saints.* To them God chose to make known *how great among the Gentiles are the riches of the glory of this mystery, which is Christ in you,* the hope of glory. *Him we proclaim, warning* every person and *teaching* every person in all wisdom, that we may present every [person] *mature in Christ.* For this I toil, striving with all the energy which he mightily inspires within me.

Here in this single passage are all the major points about the experience of being in Christ that Paul already covered in his earlier letters.

1. Sharing the passion of Christ—the true *imitatio Christi*—is the mark of the mature Christ mystic. (I Corinthians 4:10-16; 11:23-12:10; Philippians 1:20-23; 3:8-11. See also Colossians 4:3, where Paul declares that "the mystery of Christ" has led him to prison.)
2. The mystery has been hidden for ages and is now revealed to believers (I Corinthians 2:6-7).
3. The content of the mystery concerns God's plan for the salvation of Gentiles. (Romans 16:25. Also compare Colossians 3:10-11 with Galatians 3:28; in the new creation there is neither Jew nor Greek, for all are one in Christ.)
4. Those who perceive the divine revelation are in Christ and Christ is in them (*passim*).
5. Those who combine the divine revelation (ecstasy) with wise instruction (ethics) will become mature persons in Christ, which leads us back to the first point, the shared passion of Christ (I Corinthians 2:6; also in Colossians 2:2 Paul associates the "knowledge of God's mystery" with *agape.*)

And there you have it! This one passage from Paul's letter to the Colossians crystallizes the apostle's understanding of Christ-mysticism.

Paul was *the* mature person in Jesus Christ.

He is the father of all fledgling, struggling Christians who with adultlike maturity interweave ecstasy with the ethics of being in Christ and thus seek to minister in Jesus' name.

He is the father of all who, having matured in Christ, pray for the courage necessary to be full imitators of Christ and participants in his passion.

He is the father of all who know deeply within themselves that even in their mature strength, they are weak. In that inner wisdom is divine strength.

V. Paul and the Church: One in Christ

Drawing out practical considerations and applications from my own research is not my particular forte, as many of my confused students would testify. Let me simply close this study by making some observations on how over the centuries the church has appropriated, or sometimes misappropriated, Paul's Christ-mysticism.

First, there has been a tendency to raise the in-Christ experience to a cosmic level. In the letter to the Ephesians, Paul's mystical relationship with Christ was reduced to a doctrine about Christ, while the mystical "being in Christ" was expanded to being filled with God (see Ephesians 3:14-19; 5:1). I suspect that many contemporary mystics recognize a difficulty discovered by the author of Ephesians: How can one have a mystical experience of being united with a historical person? Such an experience seems so mundane, so limited. Jesus, after all, was bound by time and space. What the soul desires is contact with the eternal and infinite—ambitious! Yet, how much more difficult it is to be one with Christ—absurd![1]

Kierkegaard once noted that the preacher preaches in terms of the eternal: always, never, nothing, everything, infinite love, everlasting mercy—eternal verities for the "eighth day." But with Monday comes reality, limitation, all the problems of office, school, and shop that manage to survive Sunday unnoticed.[2] The eternal verities seem so out of reach that we stand in awe of the Taize monk, Tibetan guru, and Rosicrucian who seem to have such direct and easy access to the eternal world. The cosmic consciousness is theirs and not ours. Moreover, most of us do not live in such exotic places as Tibet, France, or California. To be in Christ may be a lower, but perhaps more attainable goal for those of us in Rochester, Buffalo, or Detroit. To be in Christ may be esoteric, but it need not be exotic.

Second, one could philosophize about being in Christ. The book of Hebrews tends to displace Christ-mysticism by philosophy.[3] Philosophizing has many advantages: anyone can do it, no special talent or insight is required, one need not risk much in the process, we can regulate the demands (temporal, ethical) that the process makes on us, and it is free. We are all philosophers—"philosophers of life." Much of our adult life is spent speaking about such abstractions as love, hate, soul, mind, life, nature—notions that remain in the abstract philosophical realm until there is a flesh and blood, earth and sky, encounter of subject with subject. Likewise, one can speculate *ad nauseum* about being in Christ as long as the concept remains "out there." Nevertheless, once I encounter what is "out there" and become a subject (subjected) to it then no amount of speculation can satisfactorily describe the experience of being in Christ. A friend of mine once said of faith that if you have it, no explanation is necessary; if you don't, no explanation is possible. So it is with the experience of being in Christ.

Third, it seems almost too easy to write of the institutionalization of the in-Christ experience. This process goes back to Paul himself—being in Christ as a *personal experience* led him to conclude that the body of Christ was the *corporate expression* of being in Christ. The Pastoral Epistles completely submerge the mystic experience into the evolving ecclesiastical institutions.[4] It is clear, however, that Paul himself did not confuse personal experience with corporate expression—nor should we. Our churches,

PAUL AND THE CHURCH

denominations, and 475 Riverside Drive may be well-meaning, responsible, and spiritually alive, but they cannot fully comprise the ethical and ecstatic dimensions of being in Christ. I have little use for individualistic, pietistic religion; we can do more together than alone. On the other hand I want *each member* of the body to be deeply in touch with the spirit that gives life to the community.

Finally, there are those—and if Greeley and McCready are correct, in greater numbers than we may suspect—who are deeply in touch with the mystical ground of Christianity. For them, cosmological absorption, doctrines about Christ, psychological fantasies, philosophical speculation, and institutional regulation—whether fundamentalist or liberal—are all inadequate. That which is a lasting and continuous source of strength and courage is a seldom but powerfully experienced awareness of one's deepest, primordial being that extends backward through time and into eternity and, at the same time, moves forward through time into eternity—the end shall be as the beginning. It is a momentary but awesome experience of being absorbed by the Infinite—being in Christ—and then released to do what needs to be done in this world. In his sermon "You Are Accepted," Paul Tillich suggests that this may be the experience of grace.

Tillich recalls that Paul of Tarsus was in his mid-thirties when in

> the picture of Jesus as the Christ, which appeared to him at the moment of his greatest separation from other men, from himself and God, he found himself accepted in spite of his being rejected. And when he found that he was accepted, he was able to accept himself and to be reconciled to others. . . .
>
> Sometimes it happens that we receive the power to say "yes" to ourselves, that peace enters into us and makes us whole, that self-hate and self-contempt disappear, and that our self is reunited with itself. Then we can say that grace has come upon us.[5]

Paul the apostle could say that, having received grace, he was a new man in Christ, absorbed by the power of the Eternal and Infinite.

I strongly believe that Paul's Christ-mysticism is available for all who are in search of the unity and reality within them. Hopefully this unity may be expanded and shared with our congregations and with our denomination so that one day all may experience the trauma and joy of becoming a new creation. This can be yet another growing dimension of our Christian life, a dimension filled with uncertainty. Remember that Paul said, "Work out your own salvation [wholeness] with fear and trembling" (Philippians 2:12). Poet e. e. cummings put it this way:

> I am someone who proudly and humbly affirms that love is the mystery-of-mysteries, and that nothing measurable matters "a very good goddamn": that "an artist, a man, a failure," is no mere whenfully accreting mechanism, but a givingly eternal complexity—neither some soulless and heartless ultrapredatory infra-animal nor any un-understandingly knowing and believing and thinking automation, but a naturally and miraculously whole human being—a feelingly illimitable individual; whose only happiness is to transcend himself, whose every agony is to grow.[6]

And it is agony. To grow and to be in touch with the mystical side of ourselves, to reach down deeply in order to discover who we are in our essence, to be related to our primordial being, is the greatest of agonies. It is agony because it is death—death to the old creation, death to the old order, death to the old man or woman, death to time and space. "Wretched man that I am!" says Paul, "Who will deliver me from this body of death?" (Romans 7:24). For Paul the agony of self-discovery was as painful as crucifixion: "I have been crucified with Christ." We carry "in the body the death of Jesus" (Galatians 2:20; II Corinthians 4:10).

Yet Paul experienced within himself not only the agony of death but the joy of new life: "For to me to live is Christ, and to die is gain. . . . I have been crucified with Christ; it is no longer I who live, but Christ who lives in me; and the life I now live in the flesh I live by faith in the Son of God, who loved me and gave himself for me" (Philippians 1:21; Galatians 2:20).

Paul was part of the newly created order in which the strained relationship between God and man had been reconciled. Paul's mystic experience of the resurrected Christ in his own life assured him that nothing temporal or spatial would separate him from the love of God. "For I am sure that neither death, nor life, nor angels, nor principalities, nor things present, nor things to come, nor powers, nor height, nor depth, nor anything else in all creation, will be able to separate us from the love of God in Jesus Christ our Lord" (Romans 8:38-39). And finally, Paul's Christ-mysticism compelled him to deal with all of creation as the new creation.

> From now on, therefore, we regard no one from a human point of view; even though we once regarded Christ from a human point of view, we regard him thus no longer. Therefore, if anyone is in Christ, he is a new creation; the old has passed away, behold, the new has come. (II Corinthians 5:16-17)

The experience of being in Christ reveals within us, often in momentary and gentle ways, a power which transcends our humanity—the power of the Eternal, the Unconditional, the Infinite, and the Ultimate.

NOTES

Introduction

1. Andrew M. Greeley and William C. McCready, "Are We a Nation of Mystics?" *New York Times Magazine*, January 26, 1975, p. 21.
2. Albert Schweitzer, *The Psychiatric Study of Jesus: Exposition and Criticism* (Boston: Beacon Press, 1948), pp. 44-45.
3. Roland Bainton, "Psychiatry and History: An Examination of Erikson's 'Young Man Luther,'" *Religion in Life*, Winter, 1971, pp. 1-2.

Chapter I

From Death to Life

1. See especially Adolf Deissmann, *Paul: A Study in Social and Religious History* (New York: Harper, 1927).
2. W. D. Davies, *Paul and Rabbinic Judaism: Some Rabbinic Elements in Pauline Theology* (New York: Harper, 1948); H. J. Schoeps, *Paul: The Theology of the Apostle in the Light of Jewish Religious History* (Philadelphia: Westminster Press, 1961).
3. Richard Rubenstein, *My Brother Paul* (New York: Harper, 1972).
4. See Gunther Bornkamm, *Paul* (New York: Harper, 1971), pp. xv-xxi.
5. Deissmann, *Paul: A Study*, p. 25.

Chapter II

Paul the Pharisee

1. Schoeps, *Paul: The Theology*, p. 17.
2. *Ibid.*, pp. 28-29.
3. See Kirsopp Lake, "Proselytes and God-fearers," in *The Beginnings of Christianity*, 5 vols. (London: Macmillan, 1932), V, 74-96. There are, of course, some writings of the Diaspora that condemn paganism. Such polemics, however, seem directed primarily to the Jewish community, encouraging Jews not to be seduced by competing religions; *cf.* the Wisdom of Solomon, IV Maccabees, and parts of the Sibylline Oracles.
4. Josephus, *Against Apion*, 123, 280-81; *Jewish War*, 7, 45; *Antiquities*, 20, 17-96.

5. Robert A. Kraft, "Judaism on the World Scene," in *The Catacombs and the Colosseum*, ed. Stephen Benko *et al.* (Valley Forge, Pa.: Judson Press, 1971), pp. 88-90.
6. The dichotomous picture I have drawn between "liberal" Diaspora and "conservative" Palestinian Judaism is an oversimplification of a long-standing scholarly debate. In 1914, C. J. C. Montefiore published *Judaism and St. Paul*, which attempted to show that the reverse was actually the case. The God of the Palestinian Jew was closer, more approachable; the Law was not a burden, but a joyful source of community life; the world was not bad, but good. Over against this view Montefiore posits Diaspora Judaism as a cold, harsh, somber religion in which God is a remote despot, the Law a source of doubt, and the material world is evil.

Recently Montefiore has been challenged by W. D. Davies. With regard to the Law, both Paul and the Palestinian rabbis understood that "the Law was to be obeyed literally, it was not merely symbolic of the great principles of Judaism as to so many Hellenistic Jews. We cannot therefore vaguely assume that such discontent with the Law as we find in Paul . . . was due to his experience in the Diaspora, for discontent was not unknown in Palestine." Davies, *Rabbinic Judaism*, p. 11.

On the nature of God in Hellenistic Judaism, scholars are confined to the primary philosophical representative, Philo of Alexandria. Even though Philo borrows philosophical concepts from Hellenism and Jewish theology, he can also make the simple comparison of God to a father. "In any case, every Jew in the Diaspora was not a Philo and it is not known how far Hellenistic philosophical ideas did influence all Greek-speaking Jews. . . . Vague generalizations about the influence of Hellenistic philosophy upon the idea of God in Paul as opposed to ideas held by Palestinian Jews are, therefore, worthless." *Ibid.*, p. 12.

With respect to the material world, it is quite true that the Aristotelian view of the universe was pervasive—that is, if one pictures the universe as a funnel, the earth lies at the bottom where it catches all the dregs of the universe. It is composed of hard, cold matter and is far removed from the ethereal realm of divinity. In rabbinic literature as well as in Philo, the holiness and purity of God are prophylactically maintained by using the "Word" as the agent of creation. There were four major ways of dealing with the problem of living in the material world: (1) by devising ways of escape (*e.g.*, through asceticism, mysticism, or gnosticism), (2) by stoically coping with the given evil situation, (3) by hedonistically denying any moral order in the universe, and (4) by developing a pantheon of intermediaries between God and the earth. Both Hellenistic and Palestinian Judaism rejected the second and third alternatives, while appropriating the first and last. The Essene communities in Palestine, the mystical experience of some Palestinian rabbis, and the development by both Hellenistic and Palestinian authorities of such divine intermediaries as the Word, the Law, and angels, all point to an attempt at transcending the distance between God and the world. This world seems to have been no less an evil place for Palestinian Jews than for Jews in the Diaspora.

Therefore, if the points of view on the major Judaic issues (Torah, God, and the world) balance out so that Hellenistic Judaism need not stand in a poor light by comparison to Palestinian Judaism, then on the basis of the subsidiary issue of the Jewish attitude toward non-Jews, I feel free to suggest that the Diaspora Judaism of Paul's childhood was more liberal, generous, and less restrictive than he might have experienced in Palestine.

7. What makes the Lucan version of the Pauline persecution even more suspect is the notion that Paul was sent as an emissary of the Jerusalem high priest. If such was the case, Luke records the only instance of such personal interference in the affairs of Diaspora Judaism by the Jerusalem leadership. "Hands off" was the policy and practice of the Palestinian Jews. See James Parkes, *The Foundations of Judaism and Christianity* (Chicago: Quadrangle, 1960), pp. 106-7.

Another minor point deserves to be mentioned: Why were the apostles allowed to remain in Jerusalem during the persecution instead of being dispersed like the rest of the church (see Acts 8:16)? It seems reasonable that if one is truly intent on destroying a movement one makes certain that the leadership is wiped out.

8. Josephus, *Antiquities*, 20, 200-203; see Samuel G. F. Brandon, *The Fall of Jerusalem and the Christian Church*, rev. ed. (London: S.P.C.K., 1968), pp. 95-100, 130-32.

Chapter III

Paul the Christian

1. Rubenstein, *Brother Paul*, pp. 34-35.
2. William James, *The Varieties of Religious Experience* (New York: Collier, 1902), pp. 157-206.
3. *Ibid.*, p. 177.
4. Lake, "The Conversion of Paul," in *Beginnings of Christianity*, V, 190.
5. *Ibid.*, V, 194-95.
6. In commenting on the Acts account of Paul's conversion, Carl Jung notes that "Paul had already been a Christian for a long time, only unconsciously; hence his fanatical resistance to the Christians, because fanaticism is only found in individuals who are compensating secret doubts. The incident . . . on the way to Damascus marks the moment when the unconscious complex of Christianity broke through into

consciousness. . . . Unable to conceive of himself as a Christian, . . . he became blind and could only regain his sight through . . . complete submission to Christianity. Psychogenetic blindness is according to my experience always due to an unwillingness to see. . . . Paul's unwillingness to see corresponds with his fanatical resistance to Christianity." Jung, *Contributions to Analytical Psychology* (New York, 1928), p. 257.
7. Reinhold Niebuhr, *Leaves from the Notebook of a Tamed Cynic* (New York: World, 1957), pp. 144-45.
8. James B. Ashbrook, *Humanitas: Human Becoming and Being Human* (Nashville: Abingdon, 1973), pp. 158, 161-62.
9. Greeley and McCready, "Nation of Mystics," p. 15.
10. Evelyn Underhill, *The Mystics of the Church* (New York: Schocken Books, 1964), p. 25.
11. *Ibid.*, p. 26. The second step in the pilgrimage is illumination, "the peaceful certitude of God, and perception of the true values of existence in His light"; the final stage is union, the "perfect and self-forgetting harmony of the regenerate will with God which makes the fullgrown mystic capable of 'being to the Eternal Goodness what his own hand is to man'. . . This is the true 'spiritual marriage' of the soul." *Ibid.*, pp. 27-28.
12. *Ibid.*, p. 13.
13. Albert Schweitzer, *The Mysticism of Paul the Apostle* (London, 1931), p. 2.
14. Mircea Eliade, *Myths, Dreams, and Mysteries: The Encounter Between Contemporary Faiths and Archaic Realities*, trans. Phillip Mairet (New York: Harper, 1960), p. 66.
15. Carl G. Jung, "Aion," in *Psyche and Symbol: A Selection from the Writings of C. G. Jung* (Garden City, N.Y.: Doubleday, 1958), pp. 35-36.
16. Schweitzer, *Mysticism*, chap. 2.
17. *Ibid.*, p. 117.
18. Albert Schweitzer, *Paul and His Interpreters* (London, 1912), p. 225.
19. See Davies, *Rabbinic Judaism*, chaps. 5, 8, for a similar perspective that links being "in Christ" with being "in the church."
20. Jung, "Aion," pp. 38, 35-36.
21. Paul's mysticism is neither a Hellenistic loss of human personality to the divine world, as Gal. 3:27-28 shows, nor a gnostic loss of human distinctions. In the church, Jews and Greeks, slaves and free, male and female, are different but equal.

Robin Scroggs' excellent article in the Sept., 1972, issue of the *Journal of the American Academy of Religion*, "The Eschatological Woman," puts to rest the notion that Paul was one of the all-time great male chauvinists. Scroggs reiterates the fact that passages portraying women as subjected to men are found in the deutero-Pauline literature. Paul himself sees women as partners in his ministry, equal in every way. There is not a shred of subjugation in I Cor. 7, and Paul's whole argument in I Cor. 11 is a defense for women's new freedom in Christ to participate fully—in worship, in study, in authority—in the life of the church.

I suspect that Paul, convinced of the equality of all humanity before God, tried desperately to turn his conviction into reality by encouraging the equal participation of women alongside men in worship, missionary activity, and church leadership. This was a concept for which the nascent church, still closely tied to the customs of the synagogue, was not yet ready. Therefore, to be more acceptable to the large Jewish population within the church, later Paulinists felt compelled to temper their master's revolutionary ideas.

Chapter IV
Paul the Person

1. The book of Acts suggests Paul's occupation. Paul's own writings are not specific; he simply states that he labored with his hands to earn his bread. Although as an apostle he deserved to be supported financially by his churches, he chose to be above reproach, especially from the Corinthians, and supported himself (see I Cor. 9:3-18; I Thess. 2:9).

Paul was anything but an impressive figure of a man. After much anguish an exhausted Paul says to the church at Corinth: "I do not even seem to frighten you with my letters, for some of you say, 'His letters are weighty and strong, but his bodily presence is weak and his speech is of no account'" (II Cor. 10:9-10). He considered himself to be repulsive as the result of a physical affliction. Even though the Galatians rejected Paul's gospel of freedom from the Law, the apostle reminded them that at the beginning of his ministry there, they did him no wrong: "You know it was because of a bodily ailment that I preached the gospel to you at first, and though my condition was a trial to you, you did not scorn or despise me, but received me as an angel of God, as Christ Jesus" (Gal. 4:13-14).

It was perhaps this angelic allusion that provoked the imaginative description in *Acts of Paul and Thecla* in the late second century. Paul was "a man small of stature, with a bald head and crooked legs, in a healthy state of body, with his eyebrows knit together and a somewhat hooked nose, full of friendliness; for on the one hand he appeared to be like a man yet on the other he had the face of an angel." Edgar Hennecke, *The New Testament Apocrypha*, 2 vols. (Philadelphia: Westminster Press, 1965), II, 353-54.

We shall never know the nature of Paul's "thorn in the flesh." Was it a speech problem, bad eyes, crooked legs, or the chairman of the board of deacons at Ephesus? Although we know little about Paul "according to the flesh," we can know something about him "according to the spirit."

2. Rubenstein, *Brother Paul*, pp. 35, 41, 37.
3. *Ibid.*, pp. 40-43, 84-85.
4. *Ibid.*, p. 40.
5. See Rudolf Bultmann, *Jesus Christ and Mythology* (New York: Scribner's, 1958), p. 48.
6. Niebuhr, *Notebook of a Cynic*, p. 222.
7. The medical term for the surgical operation is "cerebral commissurotomy." Michael Gazzaniga reports that "the demonstration in experimental animals that sectioning of the *corpus callosum* did not seriously impair mental faculties had encouraged surgeons to resort to this operation for people afflicted with uncontrollable epilepsy. The hope was to confine the seizure to one hemisphere. The operation proved to be remarkably successful." Gazzaniga, "The Split Brain in Man," in *The Nature of Human Consciousness: A Book of Readings*, ed. Robert Ornstein (San Francisco: W. H. Freeman, 1973), p. 88.

    Although the operations were successful in terms of eliminating epileptic attacks, considerable adjustment had to be made to the separate (but now equal) functioning of each half of the brain.

    Gazzaniga cites several interesting experiments. One example will do: "When the word 'pencil' was flashed to the right hemisphere, the patients were able to pick out a pencil from a group of unseen objects with the left hand. . . . When a patient held an object . . . (out of view), although he could not say its name or describe it, he was later able to point to a card on which the object was written." *Ibid.*, p. 92.
8. Robert Ornstein, *The Psychology of Consciousness* (San Francisco: W. H. Freeman, 1972), pp. 67-68.
9. See Jerome D. Frank, *Persuasion and Healing* (Baltimore: John Hopkins Press, 1963), pp. 42-43. Frank notes that one of the ways American prisoners of war of the Japanese and Koreans combatted their feelings of abandonment, hopelessness, and physical and mental decay was to arouse the anger of one another.
10. Ornstein, *Psychology of Consciousness*, p. 134.
11. Claudio Naranjo, *The Healing Journey: New Approaches to Consciousness* (New York: Ballantine, 1973), p. 17.
12. *Ibid.*, p. 39.
13. Such pedantry probably was performed by the author of Ephesians, which reads like a golden treasury of Pauline "gems of wisdom."

Chapter V

Paul and the Church

1. Sören Kierkegaard beautifully stated that "the absurd is—that the eternal truth has come into being in time, that God has come into being, has been born, has grown up . . . has come into being precisely like any other individual human being." Kierkegaard, "Concluding

Unscientific Postscript," in *A Kierkegaard Anthology*, ed. Robert Bretall (Princeton: Princeton University Press, 1946), p. 220.
2. *Ibid.*, p. 232.
3. The author appears to be influenced by the neo-Platonic idea of this world as an imperfect copy of a perfect heavenly world (see Heb. 6:1; 8:26–9:6; 10:1; 19–22).
4. See I Tim. 1:3-4, 10; 3:1, 8; 4:6; 5:17-22; II Tim. 3:14-15; Titus 1:5; 2:1.
5. Paul Tillich, "You Are Accepted," in *The Shaking of the Foundations* (New York: Scribner's, 1948), pp. 163, 160.
6. e. e. cummings, *I: Six Nonlectures* (New York: Atheneum, 1953), pp. 110-11.

PART II
ARRIVING WHERE WE STARTED: BEYOND LIBERAL CRITICISM and CONSERVATIVE COMMITMENT

James B. Ashbrook

I. Dilemma and Direction: Two Brains and Two Realms

Belief confronts us with a dilemma: What do we do with our mind? Can we think and also trust? Is it possible to risk and still reason? Can we let go and yet be logical? Are commitment and criticism compatible?

Christians often separate faith and reason. I do not nor does my co-author. We are critical in assessing beliefs. We are equally committed to believing. Whereas Walaskay has come at the dilemma through an immersion in the life and thought of one person (the apostle Paul), I come at it through an exploration of general human consciousness. In what follows I examine both difficulties and directions I regard as integral to a life of faith. The search is for that which lies beyond liberal criticism and conservative commitment.

The Dilemma

By "critical" I mean any approach that is analytical, cognitive, historical, developmental, theoretical, and abstract.[1] Abstractions are vague—that is, ideas cut off from the reality in which people live and move and have their being. Everything is questioned—except questioning!

A critical approach to faith does not satisfy our longing for experience. It collapses from too much questioning, too much dissecting, too much analyzing, It is, as Alan Watts points out, as futile as studying birdsongs in a collection of stuffed nightingales. It is as unsatisfying as reading menus in order to satisfy hunger pangs. It can lead to an arrogant detachment that is as ridiculous as it is pathetic.

Critical coolness deludes us into thinking we have life in hand, oblivious of the fact that we have nothing in hand but analysis. People look for life and end up crying out with Mary Magdalene in the garden, "They have taken away the Lord . . . and we know not where they have laid him."

To me, an uncritical counterbalance is no better. By "uncritical" I mean any approach that is accepting, emotional, immediate, self-evident, conventional, and particular. Particulars cut us off from perspective! They prevent our distinguishing trends from trivia, what is significant from what merely gratifies.

An uncritical approach to faith lacks perspective. It collapses from too much reliance on appearances and simplifications, naïveté and the conventional. At times it can lead to an ignorant involvement that would be laughable if it were not so dangerous.

The irrational, the arbitrary, the latent consequences of even our best intentions all have a way of sabotaging us. This unexpected negativity calls into question political piety, individual Puritanism, and ecclesiastical innocence. Sigmund Freud contended that we are all far more immoral than we know. Paul made the point even stronger: "There is none righteous, no, not one" (Romans 3:10 KJV).

Karl Marx corroborated what the prophets proclaimed in the name of Yahweh, namely, that socioeconomic determinism shapes ideological values (*cf.*, Jeremiah 8:10*b*-11; Isaiah 5:20-23; Amos 2:6-7*a*; 4:24; 6:1*a*–6).

DILEMMA AND DIRECTION

Uncritical faith deludes us into believing we are blessed with the Spirit. Like people in Jeremiah's time the word of the Lord comes to us, "Do not trust in these deceptive words: 'This is the temple of the Lord' . . . For if you truly amend your ways . . . if you truly execute justice . . . then I will let you dwell in this place" (Jeremiah 7:4-8).

A post-critical approach goes beyond both uncritical warmth and critical coolness. But if we are to retain the critical *and* maintain commitment, how do we avoid too much detachment on the one hand and too much immersion on the other?

A Direction

I propose using what we know of the human brain.

As a working model, the brain can expand the way we see and understand belief.[2] It lets us elaborate relationships among aspects of belief more fully. It provides a touchstone—an example and pattern—that keeps our thinking focused. Such a procedure is analogical. That is, we can use the brain as a model to reorder present knowledge as well as to generate new understanding. While we must not take the relationship of the brain and belief literally, the analogy provides a valuable and valid way to order what we see and experience.

One Brain: Two Hemispheres

While we have one brain, we have two hemispheres. At first glance they appear symmetrical, each paralleling the other with regulatory (frontal), general sensory (parietal), visual (occipital), and auditory (temporal) regions, even as we have two eyes, two lungs, two kidneys, and so on. More exact knowledge discloses distinguishable differences. The hemispheres make unequal contributions to all sensory, perceptual, and motor functions as well as in the parts played in orientation and action.[3]

The left/right asymmetries appear to be associated with activity related to the world of people in contrast to the realm of nature. Tools, various ways of communication, and the range of symbolic behavior all free us from the symmetrical patterns of the natural world. These allow flexibility in taking in, storing, retrieving, and using information in planned behavior.[4]

In general, the left hemisphere controls the right side of the body. It performs the dominant function "in the *cerebral organization of all higher forms of cognitive activity connected with speech*—perception organized into logical schemes, active verbal memory, logical thought."[5] This lateralization of speech sharply distinguishes the organization of the human brain from that of animals.[6] Because the left hemisphere affects speech, language, time-orientation, and planned regulation of activity, I call what it does *intentional consciousness*. In short, it is active, initiating our responses to the world before and apart from what the world presents to us. With it we create and shape a world.

In contrast, the right hemisphere controls the left side of the body. Until recently little was known of its contribution to distinctly human activity.[7] On its own, the right hemisphere is inadequate in naming objects, even though it can perceive directly. It processes spatial information in the third dimension—*i.e.*, depth perception—more accurately than the left hemisphere and clearly works better "in analyzing information about where objects are located in space."[8] Damage to the right hemisphere produces disturbance in recognizing objects, as well as faces, and in direct orientation in space. In addition, a person not only remains unaware of the left half of the visual field, but fails to perceive his or her own failure. In fact, the person conceals the failure by empty reasoning and excessive talking.

While not as firmly established as an understanding of the left hemisphere, what the right hemisphere does appears to be less differentiated. It takes in and analyzes direct information in regard to our own body as well as general spatial orientation. Because the right hemisphere affects perception, recognition of faces, spatial orientation, sensation, and receptive activity I call what it does *in-touch awareness*. In short, it is receptive, reacting and responding to what the world presents to us. With it we are created and shaped by the world.

The left hemisphere, controlling right-side activities, serves the cognitive functions of taking things apart, analyzing, separating, distinguishing, and manipulating in self-consciously determined freedom. It "puts out." The right hemisphere, controlling left-side activities, serves the functions of connecting, holding things together, associating, integrating, imagining, enhancing, and inspiring for an other-directed destiny. It "takes in." While both sides are capable of all brain activity, being able to compensate for cerebral deficiencies or accidents in the other side, that comes only with difficulty. By the age of three or four each side grows increasingly specialized.[9]

With the intentional left hemisphere we focus on parts and pieces and details. We see that which denotes and isolates and identifies and fixes boundaries and sets off and abstracts and generalizes and wraps up. We close off experience through specific expression.

With the in-touch right hemisphere we focus on patterns and wholes and designs. We see that which connotes and connects and unifies and wipes out boundaries and makes concrete. We are open to experience continuously.

The right hemisphere cannot say what it sees. It is basically speechless. Because of it we always know far more than we can say and even more than we can conceive. It can carry on certain activities that do not require concepts or words. It functions as a computer with its goings-on never coming into articulate expression.[10]

The left hemisphere can only say what it thinks. It is basically cognitive. Because of it we are always declaring far less than we know and much less than we imagine. It does not know or remember "anything about the experiences and activities of the other hemispheres."

The two hemispheres are connected by a group of fibers called the *corpus callosum*. These fibers correlate visual images, integrate sensations from the limbs, unify attentional processes, and provide a general tonic for the brain cells.[11]

In addition, many parts of the cerebral cortex of both hemispheres are necessary in forming and using symbols. No separate part of the brain performs the function that we call "thinking." All complex mental functions are "effected by the combined activity of both hemispheres, but each hemisphere makes its own particular contribution to the construction of mental processes."[12] The *corpus callosum* serves as an essential neurological correlate producing the experience of the singleness and unification of mental activity.[13]

Even when the hemispheres are split, they remain united via the brain stem. While factual information is not conveyed through the brainstem, emotional affects are. Thus, a person with a severed *corpus callosum* can be shown an emotion-evoking picture on the left side of a screen, intended for the right hemisphere, and the talkative left hemisphere claims it has seen nothing, even though the person reacts emotionally. Characteristically, human "consciousness resides in the tissue of both cerebral hemispheres."[14]

While there are unifying factors through feedback from activity in the body, the basic generalization that "the two brain hemispheres are for the most part separate realms of knowledge and awareness remains."[15] The left hemisphere constitutes intentional analysis; the right hemisphere, in-touch relatedness. Together they constitute one brain with unified conscious awareness.

One Reality: Two Realms

Just as there are two major divisions within our brain, there are two major realms within reality.

There is the visible world of space and time, of cause and effect, of details and description. This is the sensory world. The West has called it the "real world." In contrast, there is the invisible world of patterns and relatedness and timelessness and oneness. This is the nonsensory world. The East has known it as the "real world."

Those who emphasize the invisible world of mystery see the sensory world of mastery as illusory. On the other hand, those who emphasize the visible world of mastery view the nonsensory world of mystery as delusional.

In a fascinating investigation of the paranormal, psychologist Lawrence LeShan has clarified these two approaches to reality.[16] He organized the differences around four basic questions:

1. *What is the most important aspect of a "thing"?*
   For sensory reality it is the thing's uniqueness; for nonsensory reality it is the thing's relatedness.
2. *What is "time"?*
   For sensory reality it flows irreversibly in one direction; for nonsensory reality it is presentness without distinction of past, present, and future.
3. *How do we view "good and evil"?*
   For sensory reality experiences and issues are sifted and sorted and evaluated; for nonsensory reality experiences and issues are all received without discriminations or judgments.

THE BRAIN

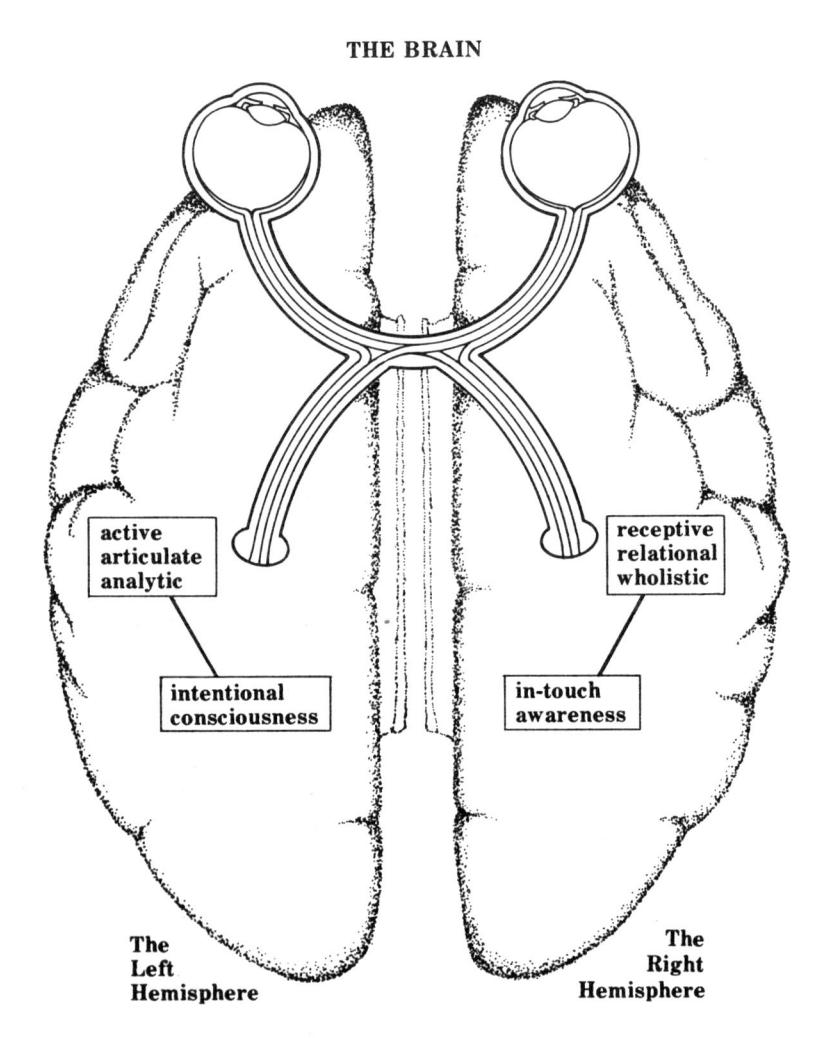

| active articulate analytic | receptive relational wholistic |

| intentional consciousness | in-touch awareness |

The Left Hemisphere

The Right Hemisphere

4. *What is the best way to gain information?*
For sensory reality it is via the sense organs; for nonsensory reality it is to accept the oneness of reality in contemplation.

Each sphere—the sphere of time and separateness and the sphere of timelessness and oneness—has its own configuration of purposes and procedures. The sensory realm accentuates multiplicity. There we select goals, plan for them, act on them, and evaluate the results. The nonsensory realm emphasizes oneness. Here we seek serenity, joy, love, and at-homeness in the cosmos.

Consequences of the Separation

Without both realms and both brains we are crippled in attaining full humanness. Like the cyclops, the gigantic one-eyed monsters of Greek and Roman mythology, we crash through the world destroying others and eventually ourselves. In the one-eyed image we see a grossly distorted self without two-way vision: the outer and the inner.

Before I lose you completely, let me remind you of my concern: post-critical faith that lies beyond liberal criticism and conservative commitment.

Critical coolness has emphasized primarily the left hemisphere. It has examined life in its pieces. In religion, the result has produced intellectuals, organizational managers, or social activists. If thinkers, they deal with ideas; if doers, they concentrate on implementation. In short, they initiate and they tackle.

Immediate experience with nonsensory reality—such as dreams, symbols, myths, imagination, prayer, mysticism—is minimized. For the sophisticate, immediate experience represents an early, irrational, immature stage of development. When one grows up, direct experience is put aside for what is rational and mature. Or so we thought.

In contrast, uncritical warmth has emphasized the right hemisphere. It has exalted life in its naturalness. In religion, the result has produced uncritical believers who declare, proclaim, direct, proselytize. If thinkers, they wait for inspired information, accenting *the* Word, *the* faith, *the* soul. If doers, they aggressively read the Bible, pray, and evangelize, stressing salvation, *the* church, *the* covenantal community. In short, they take in and stand back.

Directed action within sensory reality—for instance, against institutional oppression and collective sin—is minimized. Such corporate intentionality represents for the naïve person a denial of divine activity. Or so we thought.[17]

In contrast, I seek a sophisticated simplicity. Life is simpler than critical coolness sees. Similarly, life is more complicated than uncritical warmth believes. Neither an arrogance that reduces mystery nor a naïveté that rejects mastery is adequate.

Critical coolness overemphasizes analytical thinking in the left hemisphere and physical perception in the right hemisphere, thereby restricting itself to the sensory realm: the visible, the manageable, the intentional. It thinks too much, acts too much, attacks too much. It exaggerates what is real and relevant in the sensory realm and minimizes what is true and trustworthy in the nonsensory realm.

In contrast, ignorant warmth emphasizes received experience in the right hemisphere and fixed ideas in the left hemisphere, thereby restricting itself to the nonsensory realm: the invisible, the mysterious, the intuited, the timeless. It feels too much, submits too much, proclaims too much. It magnifies what is true and trustworthy in the nonsensory realm and dismisses what is real and relevant in the sensory realm.

The faith of pious skepticism requires that we use both sides of our brain and that we live in both realms of reality.

DILEMMA AND DIRECTION

Possibilities of the Whole

One brain argues for one reality—many-splendored in its manifestations and singularly unified in its wholeness—one God and one humanity. Intentional consciousness involves initiating, acting, evaluating, intending; in-touch awareness involves intuiting, receiving, accepting, connecting. The possibilities for a unified whole include right-hand mastery and left-hand mystery, cognitive grasp and caring attentiveness, deliberate will and delightful love. One God and one humanity make for one reality—intentionally in touch with all.

Consider now four aspects of belief in light of the model of one brain with two minds and one universe with two realms: the Bible, God, prayer, and Christ. The Bible grounds us in the history of a people. God—the theological—orients us to the meaning of experiences and events within the scheme of things. Prayer opens the experiential and the transcendent. Christ focuses devotion, decision, and direction.

Suddenly, religious convictions baptize my secular orientation. In the end, criticalness is subservient to faith. Finally, questioning ends in commitment. T. S. Eliot expressed this in *Four Quartets*.

> We shall not cease from exploration
> And the end of all our exploring
> Will be to arrive where we started
> And know the place for the first time.

Beyond ignorant warmth and arrogant coolness lies a whole faith, personal and prophetic, that brings us back to where we began, namely, the living Lord in the New Jerusalem, where God becomes all in all, dwelling within us intuitively and incarnate among us intentionally. We live beyond the divorce of piety and skepticism.

| HUMANITY | GOD | REALITY |

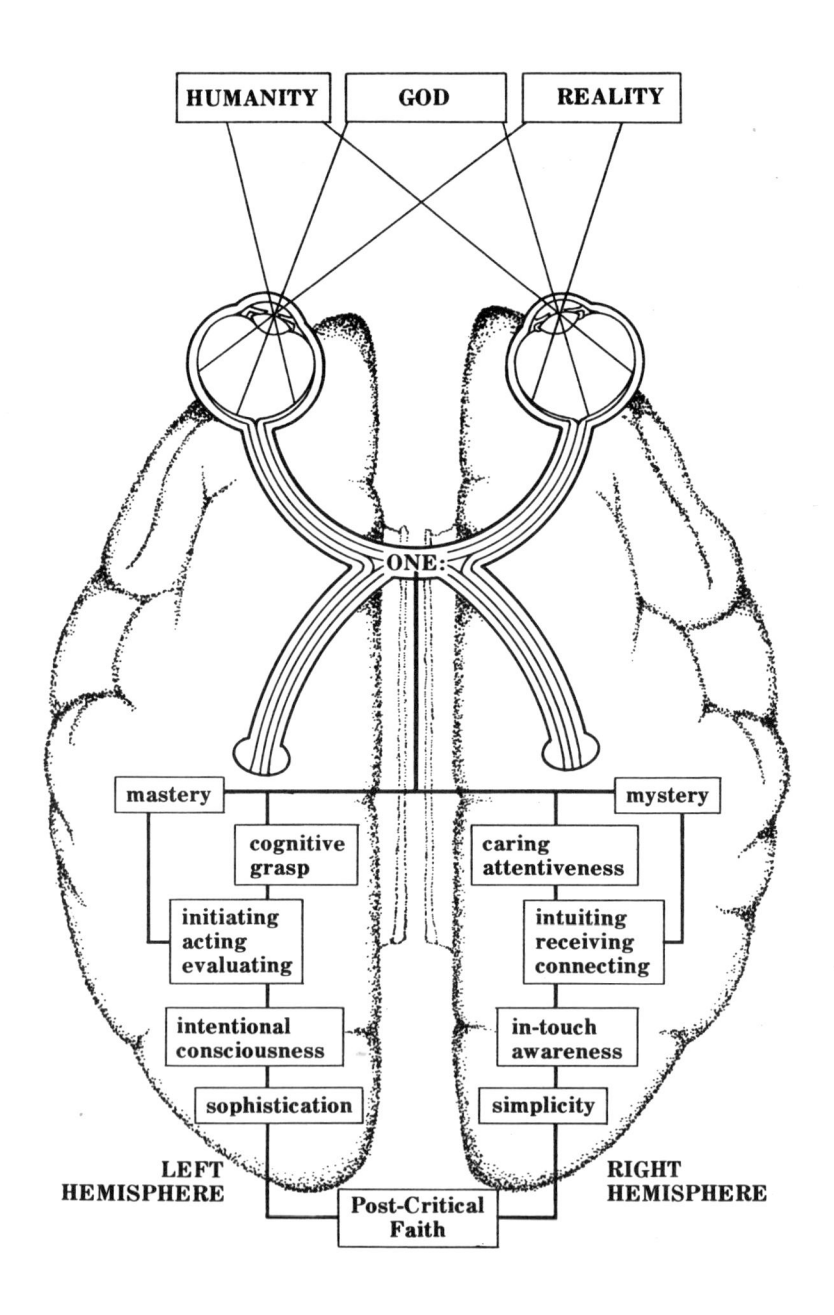

ONE:

LEFT HEMISPHERE		RIGHT HEMISPHERE
mastery		mystery
cognitive grasp		caring attentiveness
initiating acting evaluating		intuiting receiving connecting
intentional consciousness		in-touch awareness
sophistication		simplicity
	Post-Critical Faith	

II. Using the Bible: Penetrating and Participating

Occasionally I ask myself: To what do I refer most often for images, ideas, insights, and illustrations of what matters? The answer is clearly the Bible.

The approach is pragmatic.

Nevertheless, intellectual honesty compels me to ask whether what I find valuable can have validity for others. Uncritical warmth, in my view, disregards the validity issue by making "This is truth for me" equal "This is truth for all." On the other hand, critical coolness goes after facts to the loss of the meaning of facts, *i.e.*, what is valuable.

The issue in understanding the Bible is this: Can one be critical of the words yet faithful to the Word? Can a post-critical use of scripture take into account the question of validity and the matter of value?

The Critical Heritage

In a critical approach to Bible we are indebt to Origen (*ca.* A.D. 185-254), that greatest of ante-Nicaean Fathers. He spoke of the "impossible" and the "unreasonable" character of taking some of the scripture literally:

> What [person] of intelligence will believe that the first and the second day and the third day, the evening and the morning existed without the sun and moon and stars? . . . And who is so silly as to believe that . . . one could partake of "good and evil" by masticating the fruit taken . . . from the tree of that name? And when God is said to "walk in the paradise in the cool of the

day" and Adam to hide himself behind a tree, I do not think anyone will doubt that these are figurative expressions which indicate certain mysteries through a semblance of history and not through actual events.[1]

But in the headiness of discovering such discernible threads as the Pentateuchal sources (J,E,P, and D), two or three sources of the Synoptic Gospels, and the fact that some of the Pauline corpus was not written by Paul, or in the reasonableness of rejecting the absurdity of spontaneous pregnancy and the resuscitation of a decaying corpse, a critical approach can unintentionally cut itself off from the source of its soul.

Origen sensed the danger of using critical tools to discover the heart of the gospel.[2] For him analytical tools such as literature, grammar, and geometry constituted the spoils of Egypt. They were fair game within the theological enterprise. But these "spoils" had value only if a person brought them back to the Holy Land to use for building the temple of the Lord. Origen contended that the critical approach must always be "controlled and held in subjection," for "rare is the [person] who succeeded in taking from Egypt only its useful things, and then going away to employ them for the service of God." One could too easily be encumbered by useless or even destructive tools.

Today, the dividends of such insights have ceased. The assets of critical clarity are exhausted. Biblical criticism is "bankrupt." What happened?[3] According to those more expert than myself, its methodology is inadequate, its objectivism is false, its technology is uncontrolled, its community is sterile, its usefulness is past. I simply state these charges without taking time to elaborate them to suggest that biblical criticism has generated as much difficulty for faith as it has resolved. Yet the critical intent must never be abandoned—namely, to make words sure and the Word significant. That task is always necessary!

So, if criticism frees us to use the Bible, what might a post-critical approach be like?

At a crucial juncture, Origen and the Alexandrian school of biblical interpretation enabled thoughtful Christians to uphold the rationality of faith.[4] They did it through the use of the allegorical method that looked for hidden meaning in every word of the Bible (even at the expense of the context of a text and the "reality" of events).[5] I find the approach suggestive.

The Alexandrian School explored three levels of meaning: (1) a "bodily meaning" or literal sense, (2) the "soul meaning" or moral and ethical sense, and (3) the "spiritual meaning" or allegorical-mystical sense. As Origen wrote, "The impossibility of the literal sense turns one to an examination of the inner meaning."[6] I regard the concrete (literal) level as the historical stage that grounds the issues of validity and value in the world around us. The psychological (soul) level, or the personal stage, opens these issues to the world within us. Finally, the spiritual level, or the cosmic stage, connects validity and value to the universe beyond us. Each stage or level contributes to our understanding.

A class on Herman Melville conveys my intent. The teacher dismissed a student's insistence on dealing with *Moby Dick* when the discussion was on *Billy Budd* by sneering, "I'm not interested in fish."

I contend that surrounding the realm of the concrete—or the literal, if you will—whale as fish is the intrapsychic or psychological realm in which fish, whale, water, and swallowing symbolize the unconscious of individuals as well as of humanity itself. The capture of the Leviathan with the sevenfold tackle of the line of David, with the crucifix as bait, conveys the workings of reconciliation.

As a symbol, the fish expresses many meanings.[7] It refers to fish *qua* fish, yet human imagination (seemingly

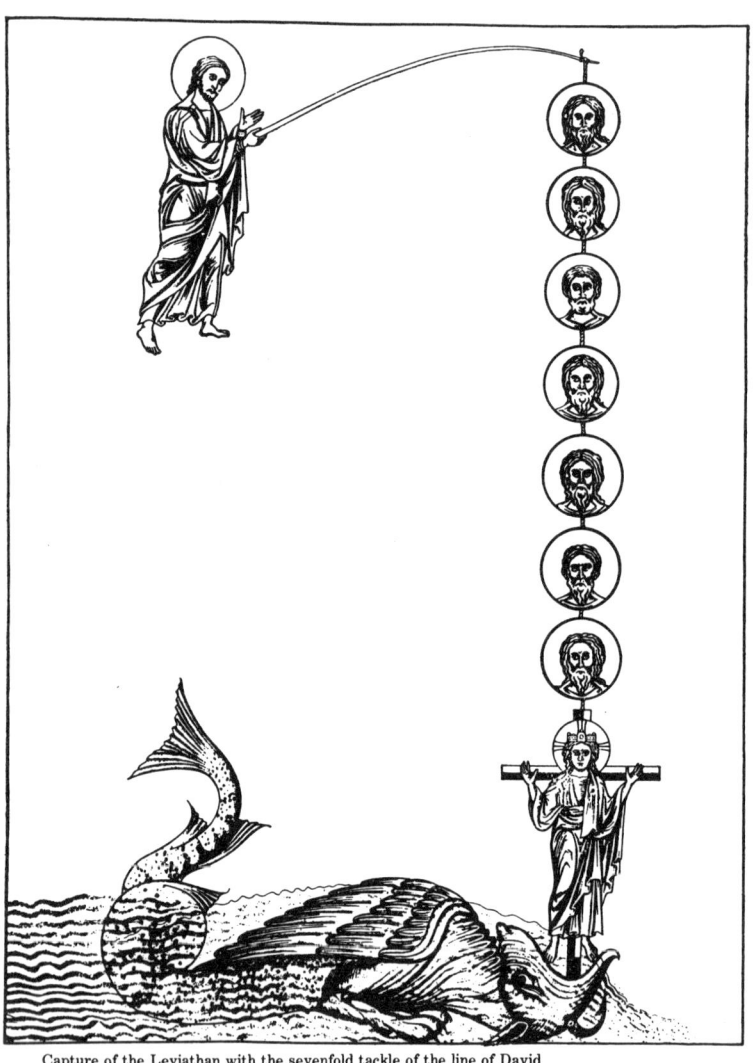

Capture of the Leviathan with the sevenfold tackle of the line of David
—Herrad of Landsberg's *Hortus deliciarum* (twelfth century)
Courtesy of the New York Public Library
Astor, Lenox and Tilden Foundations

lacking in that teacher discussing *Billy Budd*) has never left it at that. In the empirical realm we often speak of "fishing for the facts." Because fish spawn large numbers of eggs, the Babylonians, the Phoenicians, the Assyrians, and the Chinese regarded it as a symbol of sexuality infused with spirituality. As Pisces, the last of the Zodiac signs, the fish figure heralds cyclic regeneration and mystic fusion.

Under persecution the early Christians used the letters of the Greek word for fish, *ichthys*, as a secret sign of recognition: *I-esous, X-ristos, Th-eos, Y-ios, S-oter*—Jesus, Christ, God, Son, Savior. It also conveyed the life of the spirit, that realm of reality lying beneath the realm of appearances, with the fish symbolizing the life-force surging upward.

Fish and fishing disclose the struggle and resources of our human predicament. Jesus Christ calls us to become fishers of people for the saving of souls (Matthew 4:19; Luke 5:10). Fishing includes casting nets into the nonconscious of our inner world in search of understanding. We pull meaning and power out of the depths—that is, spirit. Fishing *for* souls quite simply means knowing how to fish *in* souls.

The fish expresses a psychically significant creature living in water, and water symbolizes dissolution of the old life and regeneration or resurrection in the new. Not surprisingly, Christians termed the baptismal bath a *piscina*, or "fish pond." The fish symbol thus bridges the psychic nature of humanity and the historical reality of Christ.

It is not enough to cite Origen and suggest levels of meaning in a fish for a post-critical use of the Bible. More specifically, I turn to the model of one brain with two minds, one universe with two realities. The model rejects any artificial distinction between faith and reason. For me, it includes both intentional consciousness and in-touch awareness.

Intentional Consciousness

By "intentional consciousness" I mean the systematic identification of core experiences and interpretive clues. This is an analytical penetration of the words that calls on our ability to reason, to think, to discriminate. We are to make explicit the heart of the matter, the core of the gospel, the center of its soul.

Analytical Penetration

An analytical penetration of the words exposes two core experiences around which all else cluster. One is Exodus, the other Easter. Paul speaks of these as liberation from the bondage of sin and death (Romans 8:2). In sin, we are dragged down by the oppressiveness of what has been—bondage to the past. In death, we are held back by the apprehensiveness of what is to come—bondage to the future.

> Exodus confronts us with freedom and its dizzy possibilities.
> Easter discloses destiny and its doubtful actuality.

Everything related to history, to becoming, to the drag of the past, clusters around the Exodus experience. Everything reflective of the eternal, of being, of the dread of the future, clusters around the Easter experience. Like the two hemispheres of the brain and the two realms of reality, Exodus and Easter are two manifestations of one universe and one reality. Though these experiences are distinct, they interpenetrate.

Interpretive Clues

From these core experiences, certain interpretive clues emerge. These four clues aid our liberation from the drag of the past and the dread of the future. They provide cognitive handles to make sense of confusing experiences.

First is the fundamental clue of *reversibility*. Psalm 118 presents a key image: "The stone which the builders rejected has become the chief corner-stone. This is the LORD's doing" (verse 22 NEB). That clue has shown itself to be accurate descriptively. Again and again those on the margins of life's stage turn out to be chief actors at the center of life's drama. When Mary learns that she carries the future in her womb, she also learns that the proud are scattered in the imagination of their hearts, the mighty are put down from their thrones, and those of low degree are exalted (Luke 1:51-52). The established are denied and the outcasts are acknowledged.

Such reversibility takes many forms.

—From tragedy to transformation, as with Joseph's brothers selling him into slavery and in the end Joseph telling them, "You meant to do me harm; but God meant to bring good out of it" (see Genesis 45:5 NEB).

—From the height of conquest to the humbling of pride, as with Nebuchadnezzar's dream of the mighty tree cut down; its branches lopped off, leaves stripped, and fruit thrown away; and animals fleeing from its shelter and birds from its branches (Daniel 4:7-34).

—From Amos' vision of a basket of ripened fruit and Yahweh's declaration that "my people Israel is ripe for destruction" (Amos 8:1-3 JB).

—From Paul's discoveries that "when I am weak, then I am strong" (II Corinthians 12:10 NEB) and that the wise turn out to be foolish and the foolish turn out to be wise (Romans 1:22; I Corinthians 13:18).

—From crucified, dead, and buried to triumphant, alive, and renewed.

So the examples abound. The powerful dialectic of reversibility moves through time and space.

The physical bears the weight of the psychic. From his middle-class security Nicholas Berdyaev once observed, "Bread for myself is a material question, bread for my neighbor is a spiritual question." Thus, the reality of the nonsensory bears the weight of the sensory: "Inasmuch as you do it not unto one of the least of these my family, you do it not unto me" (Matthew 25:40, author's paraphrase).

Set alongside that the fact that the physical cannot make up for the lack of the psychic. Thus Paul declares, "If I dispose of all that I possess, yes, even if I give my own body to be burned, but have no love, I achieve precisely nothing" (I Corinthians 13:3 Phillips).

Here is the coincidence of opposites in an ongoing process—from in to out, from ignorant to illumined, from the physical to the psychic. So the reversals come, the reversals go, and while we are never taken completely unaware, we are constantly surprised. Thus, the fundamental clue is reversibility.

A second interpretive clue I call *connectability*. Whether we are looking at the cause-and-effect relationship in the physical realm or the amazing configuration of meaningful coincidences in the psychic realm, which Jung called "synchronicity," connections are present. All things—unfortunate as well as fortunate, painful as well as pleasurable, dark as well as light, full as well as empty—are related or relatable to our being human. Nothing need be wasted; everything is usable in our becoming the human beings that we are. "In everything," declares Paul, "we know [that God] co-operates for good with those who love [him] and are called according to his purpose" (Romans 8:28 NEB).

While everything may not be desirable—sin and death, tragedy and injustice—everything can be drawn into the mighty work of showing forth the kingdom of love and light. While nothing can be sufficient in itself—freedom and destiny, triumph and righteousness—everything is necessarily tied in with our becoming genuinely human. No matter how desperate a situation, the question can always be asked: To what end can this be used? How is this salvageable within the economy of God's kingdom?

The negative provides energy for the positive. Being arises from the nonbeing that it resists. "Nonbeing," as Tillich saw, "drives being out of its seclusion. It forces it to affirm itself dynamically." Conversely, the negative derives its existence from the positive. Nonbeing depends upon the being that it negates for its reality. Every actual negation includes an implicit affirmation of itself in order to negate itself.[8]

In the last analysis nothing can be isolated from all other things nor can any experience be closed off as a finished event. Everything bears within it unsuspected relatedness and unexpected surprises. All that comes is related and used in a cause-and-effect way or else is relatable and usable in a psychically meaningful way. Whether causal or meaningful, there is a connectability in the "really real."

A third clue of liberation from the drag of the past and the dread of the future is what I call *vulnerability*. To be vulnerable is to let go of control and consciousness, to give up security and certainty, and to plunge into the unknown. Conventionally, we can call this the risk of faith, but too often, I fear, the batter of trust hardens into the crust of belief. So I generally prefer "vulnerable" to "faith."

Again the clue of vulnerability pervades biblical experience. Abraham, the prototype of the faithful person, went out to receive his inheritance, not knowing where he was to go (Hebrews 11:8-15). He journeyed in the midst of promise as a stranger and an alien, one not at home when he was in truth at home. He lived constantly on the road even while he struggled to settle down. And at the end of the journey, drawing his last breath, he died not having received what was promised, but having glimpsed it from afar. Abraham illustrates the life of faith: uncertain, uncomfortable, unsettled, incomplete—vulnerable, if you will.[9]

When I would save my life (which means my ego, my self-consciousness), then I am sure to lose it. To hang on is to lose out. Only in a total vulnerability—giving up every vestige of digging in and staying put and not being moved—are we liberated from past destructiveness and future disaster. Only in total vulnerability are we able to live fully and responsively in the ever-present present. Even though we are changed, we respond!

A fourth clue (and, as I said earlier, these numbers are arbitrary) balances reversibility, connectability, and vulnerability. I call this *expendability*. It appears most fully in the kenotic theory of Philippians 2.[10] Jesus, "who had always been God by nature, did not cling to his privileges as God's equal, but stripped himself of every advantage," "emptied himself" (RSV), "made himself nothing" (NEB), "by consenting to be a slave by nature and being born a man. And, plainly seen as a human being, he humbled himself" and, as the Revised Standard Version affirms, "became obedient unto death, even death on a cross" (Philippians 2:5-8 Phillips).

This affirms the self-emptying of the Creator, the incarnate, crucified Redeemer. We may think of this as the unique psychic possibility revealed in Jesus as the Christ. One gives up one's power to establish and defend one's presence. One rejects arbitrary authority that demands recognition and subservience. Not only does one let go and become vulnerable; even more, one gives up and becomes empty, void of all substance. No prominence needs pursuing, no power needs maintaining.

Even though one has a solid claim, one does not cling to prerogatives. Nor does one count on one's reputation even though it is significant. One strips oneself of privilege and becomes as nothing (no thing)—indistinguishable, undifferentiated, unrecognizable. One forgoes one's rightful claim to acknowledgment in the realm of the physical. One gives up one's rightful certainty of recognition in the realm of the psychic. One is nothing!

I have elaborated intentionally conscious ways of using the Bible by focusing on two themes and four interpretive clues. Around Exodus and freedom cluster experiences of the drag of the past. Around Easter and destiny cluster experiences of the dread of the future. The interpretive clues of reversibility, connectability, vulnerability, and expendability disclose these basic liberations.

This is mostly left-hemispheric. What of the in-touch awareness of the right hemisphere?

In-Touch Awareness

In contrast to active analysis, receptive awareness attends to imaginative participation. Here again we keep before us the two realities—the sensory realm with its concrete, historical, physical substantialness and the nonsensory realm with its suggestive, meaningful, psychic significance.

I stress the sensory realm because imaginative participation must never be an escape from the outer realm of time to an inner realm of eternity. In-touch awareness means first and always in touch with the text—with its time, its setting, its people, its development, its sources. As much as we are able, we ascertain the purposes for which the material was used within the community of faith.

As far as I am concerned, "post-critical" must be taken in the literal sense of the term—*after* criticism, not *apart* from criticism![11] The objective task isolates, identifies, and restrains our imagination and flights of fantasy. There are limits to the meanings latent in the material.

The sensory realm grounds us in history. It maintains the centrality of the whole created world. Without it we would live in an illusory world of our own imaginings.

Imaginative Participation

Along with the historical penetration of how the data came to be, we can enter into it more fully as an *outer expression* of people's *inner experience*. That includes our own inner experience as well. In that task I find understanding dreams helpful.[12]

In the dream, every part expresses some part of ourselves. We are author, stage, props, actors, audience, critic. The drama mirrors our disturbances and expresses our directions. In each object and through every action we are reconciling that which has been neglected or disowned. In truth, the dream is a vehicle of centeredness that works on our becoming whole.

In the biblical drama, therefore, every part expresses some part of humanity. The drama reflects human disturbance and discloses divine direction. In each object and through every action God is reconciling that which has been torn apart. In truth, the Bible witnesses to the redeeming Word at work in the world.

Again, in the dream, each portion must converse with every other one for reconciliation and integration. Through the dialogue the implicit is made explicit, the overlooked becomes obvious, the empty void appears pregnant with possibility.

Thus, a Jacob must face an Esau, a Gomer must talk with a Hosea, a taxcollector must deal with a zealot, a Saul is confronted by the Christ. Similarly, a wilderness desert must converse with a wandering tribe, a devouring whale must talk with a resisting Jonah, a piece of land must deal with a Jeremiah in the midst of a seige, a paralytic is confronted by the pool at Bethesda. Examples abound.

In the second account of creation in Genesis, for instance, the curious, seeking, responding "Eve" part of us must be expressed as fully as the controlling, ordering, regularizing "Adam"; the assertive, disrupting "serpent" part of us must deal with the accommodating, knowing "tree"; the purposive, integrating "Yahweh" part of us confronts those splintered selves, throwing us out of the parental womb of undifferentiated innocence into the world where our eyes are opened, we know we are seen, and we must decide who we are.

Or again, in the parable of the prodigal son, the cautious, calculating, complaining, conventional older side of us must come to terms with the carefree, uncalculating, spontaneous, unconventional younger side of us; the stabilizing, centering, integrating, enhancing creator side of us works to make whole that which has been torn apart as a result of inner alienation.[13]

In every instance—person with person, group with group, person with animal, lion with lamb, right hand with left, eye with foot, angel with animal—we enter imaginatively into the pieces. Piece confronts piece. Each part declares its presence. Each particular detail elaborates its specialness. Out of the accusing and defending, in the midst of the clashing, and because of the conversing, unexpected complementarity and commonality emerge. Each part stands forth as necessary, no part remains sufficient in itself. We see more than meets the eye.

In contrast to the method of free association—letting our imagination roam where it will—amplification of each part is a method of centered enlargement of meaning. In it we keep as close as possible to the images and ideas of the text itself. We make salient parts explicit to create the background against which the specifics are seen. We identify what the parts mean to us. We find references in literature and myths that broaden our understanding. In addition, we want to know why the material has been presented. We assume it is part of the drama of making whole the fragmented potential of ourselves and others.

New Testament scholar Walter Wink's line of questioning about the story of the healing of the paralytic (Matthew 9:1-8) illustrates one kind of amplification.[14] The questions show how we can identify various parts of ourselves with various elements in the text: "Who is the 'paralytic' in you? Who is this 'scribe' in you? Why doesn't the 'scribe' want the 'paralytic' healed—both in you *and* in the story? How are the 'paralytic' and the 'scribe' related?" Such questions press connections between our own life situation and the life demand of the gospel.

As we sharpen pieces and become the parts, we come to a final stage. Neither analytical penetration nor imaginative participation ends in itself. We take apart for the sake of putting together! In using the Bible, we realize we are called upon to use our whole head.

Compelling Imperative

From the penetration and through the participation a constellation of images and insights and ideas emerges that bursts forth as an imperative. Having struggled to find what the text does to us, we are driven to ask what are we to do with the text: "This do and you shall live." As Sören Kierkegaard insisted, the Bible is a letter from God with our individual address on it. The words are directed to *me*. I am compelled to do something! The words are directed to *you*. You are compelled to do something!

Beyond the physical and the psychic looms the spiritual: Go! Act! Do! Be! Become! Turn about! Be born anew! Using the Bible always brings us to living responsively.

"Here ends the lesson, now begins the living."

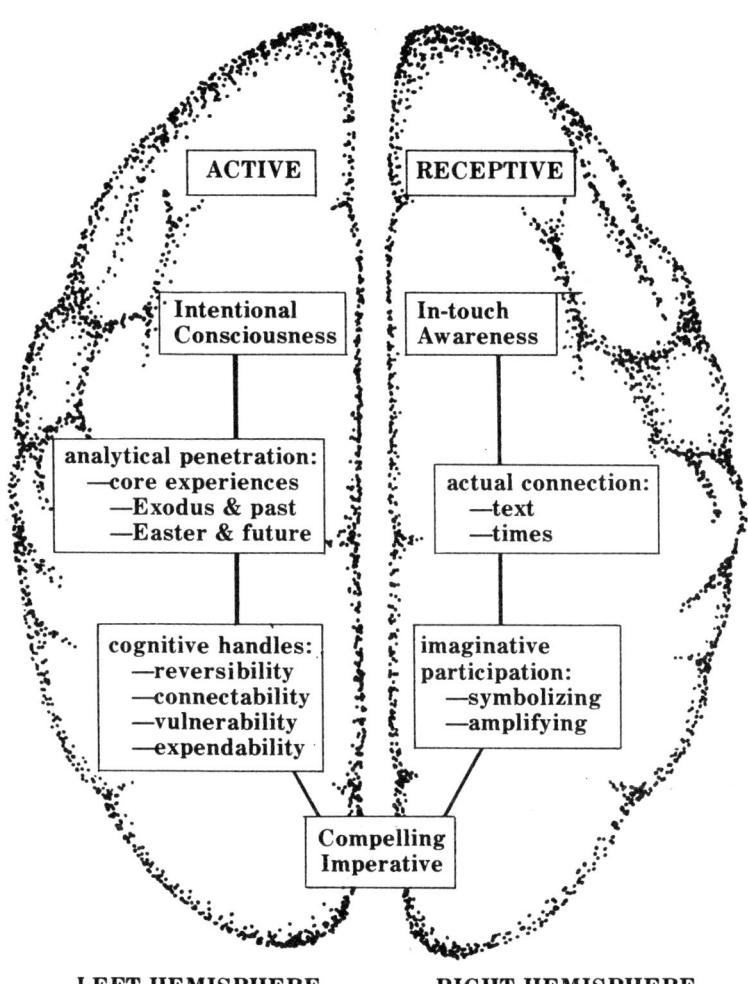

```
                    ACTIVE        RECEPTIVE

                  Intentional      In-touch
                  Consciousness    Awareness

              analytical penetration:   actual connection:
                —core experiences        —text
                —Exodus & past           —times
                —Easter & future

              cognitive handles:       imaginative
                —reversibility         participation:
                —connectability          —symbolizing
                —vulnerability           —amplifying
                —expendability

                            Compelling
                            Imperative

        LEFT HEMISPHERE          RIGHT HEMISPHERE
```

III. Speaking of God: Basis and Content

To use the Bible raises a question: Why bother with it at all?

Harvey Cox puts the issue pointedly: "Exodus and Easter add up to a vision of 'God' as whatever it is within the vast spectacle of cosmic evolution which inspires and supports the endless struggle for liberation, not just from tyranny but from all bondages."[1] I believe Exodus and Easter do add up to a vision of God. Therefore, in using the Bible, we are forced to speak of God.

But how can we speak, and what can we say?

Recent Theology

During the 1960s radical theology insisted that we could say little. In its various forms it spoke stammeringly about God and eventually fell silent. There was nothing to talk about. Instead of a pessimistic nihilism, however, it acclaimed an optimistic secularism.[2]

Radical theology called us to turn to the world—to see and sense the possibility in the secular. It reminded us that the world is our dwelling place—the here and now of this place and time. Whatever we say about God, we must include the concrete, the human, the worldly, the empirical, the sensory. Despite its excesses, radical theology warned against speaking about God too abstractly or too easily.

In the 1970s liberation theology speaks confidently of God. It calls for and celebrates liberation from oppression, especially male chauvinism and Western whiteness. Black and Third World theologies criticize the Western whitewashing of ultimate mystery and human meaning. Feminine theology calls into question the masculinization of ultimate meaning and human mystery. Rather than an optimism about the culture (religious or secular), liberation theology proclaims a radical critique.

In the hands of white, Western males, God-talk has meant conquest activity: crusades, inquisitions, witchhunts, power plays hidden under the mask of courtship, the exclusion of those who differ or are different from an elitist Kingdom in which the "most" power equals the "best" power. Despite its excesses, liberation theology challenges domesticated God-talk. Whatever else we say when we talk of God, we must include every group and every person.

Yet, I am dissatisfied with the radicals for saying nothing about God. I am equally dissatisfied with the liberationists for saying too much about God. I would like a bit more *chutzpah* (gutsiness) on behalf of God by the radicals and a little less *hubris* (pride) on behalf of their own groups by the liberationists.[3] I acknowledge Augustine's dilemma: "What can any [person] say when[one] speaks of [God]? But woe to them that keep silence—since even those who say most are dumb."

For me, to speak of God is to clarify what is and to act on what matters in being human. To speak of God is to ask:

> What is ultimate and what is urgent?
> What is real and what is right?
> What is trustworthy and what is true?

In short, to ask about God is to struggle with what matters most!

I turn again to the model of one brain with two minds. What help, if any, can it give in speaking of and about God post-critically?

The intentional consciousness of the left hemisphere must somehow combine with the in-touch awareness of the right. Attention focused on order and logic and reason must combine with attention atuned to all that is. We are obligated to what is true by our embeddedness in what is real. Our embeddedness in reality discloses to us what is trustworthy. This disclosure of what is trustworthy directs us to what is right. And the discovery of what is right brings us full circle back to what is true.

Basis for Speaking

What we say about God must be based on what we see: first experience, then expression.

Descriptive Language

When we talk of God, we are to use words descriptively. That is, words are to have contact with what is accessible to everyone—to empirical givens. In insisting upon some factual reference, I do not mean a narrow empiricism that restricts what we see and reduces what we say to physical causality, as science is popularly understood, but rather to what Ian Ramsey has termed "a wider empiricism" in which facts are inaccessible, yet have a factual reference.[4] We appeal to aspects of experience that can be shared and discussed. There is a universal quality to which we point.[5]

One factual reference lies in our existence as we know it in its full subjectivity. In the experience of ourselves—our "I-ness"—we find that which eludes direct description. At the same time we find that which is most immediately concrete. Consciousness of self is primary reality.

In other words, there is no demonstrably identifiable, particular, spatial, temporal object that is "I." "I" is not an entity, yet it has reality. In beginning with our own consciousness, we discover "something which is all of these (particular) facts and more, and [that "I"] is *not* a more that will ever be covered by more of the facts."[6]

Brain physiologist J. C. Eccles cites C. S. Sherrington to

the effect that there is no "centralization upon one pontifical nerve cell." Eccles goes on to state that "the antithesis must remain that our brain is a democracy of ten thousand million nerve cells, yet it provides us with a unified experience."[7] Our own consciousness constitutes the primary reality from which all else derives.

Another factual reference follows. It is just as elusive and just as immediate. I refer to an undifferentiated ever-present context. Here is an indwelling "am-ness." Michael Polanyi points to this when he speaks of knowledge as personal.[8] There is a "tacit dimension"—a grounding—that is wordless and inarticulate. That realm provides the raw material for what is sensed, seen, and said. Yet that realm is so rich and vast that we never begin to say what we know or understand the implications in what we say.

We actually experience but a fraction of the world bombarding us. The image of an animated cartoon of the tiniest details projected with incredible speed suggests the immensity of pattern responses spreading through the neuronal pathways in the brain. This background "noise" supports activation of attention necessary to maintain consciousness. Yet we must distinguish this background activity from foreground attention.

We direct our attention to a very select part of the sensory input. Yet without this complicated neuronal input as raw material we could not respond with awareness, recognition, comparison, value judgments, correlations with other experiences, aesthetic evaluations, and so on.[9] Polanyi views this subcortical activity as "subsidiary awareness," which is the basis of all explicit knowledge.[10] Conscious knowledge can never be made "wholly explicit." In the subsidiary awareness of particulars we discover a kind of order that goes far beyond our understanding and our ability to create.

We always know more than we can say, we always say

less than we know. Just as an ocean "waves," so the universe "peoples." But the waves are of the ocean, in the ocean, and by the ocean, and humanity is of the universe, in the universe, and by the universe.

In brief, factual reference includes consciousness of the "I" and awareness of the "am." The "I-consciousness" reflects the active, intentional left hemisphere. In contrast, the "am-awareness" reflects the receptive, intuitive right hemisphere.

Beyond the "I" and the "am" lies an "other" or a "more." "More" is not quantitative; no addition of numbers equals it. "Other" is indescribable; no precision of language captures it. That "other" or "more" than ourselves is analogous to the two hemispheres and the one brain, to the two realms and the one reality. Otherness, or "more-ness," is the situation that Ramsey labeled as "cosmic disclosure," "an awareness of objective transcendence," the circumstances in which "the universe 'comes alive,' where a 'dead,' 'dull,' 'flat' existence takes on 'depth' or another 'dimension' . . . and in it the whole universe confronts us, . . . a single individuation expressing itself in each and all of these disclosures. In other words, from any and every cosmic disclosure we can claim to believe in one (reality) . . . precisely because we talk of there being 'one world,'" even as we can refer to "one brain."[11] Here is a reality that transcends the subjective immersion of right-hemisphere receptivity and the objective restriction of left-hemisphere activity.

"God," insisted Clement of Alexandria (*ca.* A.D. 150-215), "cannot be embraced in Words or by the Mind."

Directive Language

At some point we leap from part to whole as descriptive language becomes directed language, and the mathematics of meaning move from 1/2 + 1/4 + 1/8 + 1/16 to one. Or, in the imagery of Deuteronomy 33:27, "underneath are the everlasting arms." In other words, "what there is" can never be restricted or reduced to "what is there." There is more than we see or sense. On the edges of our I-consciousness a sense of ultimacy gives perspective. In the center of our am-awareness a sense of urgency provides focus.

The words we use not only tell about reality, they also suggest how we are to act in and with reality. Descriptions, in effect, embrace directions. "The freedom of the subjective person to do as [one] pleases is averted by the freedom of the responsible person to act as [one] must."[12] We are, as Ian Ramsey points out, like musicians. We analytically understand the score; on the other hand, we emotionally give ourselves to playing it. Thereby, we respond to the disclosure that the score evokes. So, our talk of God requires that we see what is there and play what it means.

But that move from description to directive is always a leap. A gap separates what we sense from what it means. Our "I" distinguishes what we see from how it matters.

When we look at the sensory realm of time and space, we see great contrasts: order and disorder, possibility and actuality, promise and panic. We are both in touch and out of touch. Life is crucial, yet complex. Often we know that we are here, yet we are confused over what is happening. Without a sense of knowing—a design, a theme, a pattern, a gestalt—we are left with only headaches and heartaches. We find ourselves at the mercy of anything and everything.

To speak of God, therefore, is to say what matters about what is, as well as to say what is about what matters. To speak of God is to give content to convictions.

Saying and Understanding

Originally, to say something meant to "bring it into the light."[13] That is, in speaking we are showing that to which our words refer. "If nothing is expressed or represented, nothing is brought to light." So, to speak of God means to bring to light and make accessible empirical references that describe the viewable *as well as* to bring to light and make accessible experiential inferences that enlarge the knowable. To speak of God means to deal with the real, namely, what is ultimate and what is urgent!

Elements of Speaking

We must say what we discover of the ultimately real.[14] Here our understanding directs us with the in-touch awareness of the right hemisphere. We may refer to this as "evocative commitment"—impact, inspiration, passion. We love God and what God is for.

Likewise, we are required to say what we discern of the urgently right. Here our knowledge directs us with the intentional consciousness of the left hemisphere. We may term this "cognitive discernment"—content, focus, illumination. We see God and what God is about.

In speaking of God, therefore, we bring to light and make accessible that which affirms our being and inspires our destiny. There is, contended Alfred North Whitehead, "a sense of values within the structure of being."[15] The universe does indeed come alive—opening itself to us and our becoming, compelling us to see more than we want to see, challenging us to speak differently than we are wont to speak. The universe intends that we be larger, freer, more loving than we have in fact been.[16] Not only is there content in the ultimacy of the real, there is also commitment to the urgency of the right. God's justice combines with God's love. We live in light of inclusive reality.

Directions for Speaking

If the critical skeptic says too little about God and the uncritical believer says too much, a post-critical person must say something.

Clement spoke of God as not being "in space, but above both space, and time, and name, and conception." When Moses asked to know the name of Reality so that he could say something to others, he simply learned: I am/I am that I am/I am here/really present/responding/ready to respond. As Erich Fromm interprets Moses' encounter, "Unlike a thing that has reached its final form, here was Nameless Name—the name of four letters and no vowels—'living process.'"[17] Previously, whatever worked at freeing people bore another name than Yahweh. "I appeared to Abraham, to Isaac, and to Jacob, as God Almighty, but by my name the LORD I did not make myself known to them" (Exodus 6:2-3). Within the Pentateuchal tradition, the name for God changed many times. Only in its latest period did the name "God" or "Elohim" appear.[18]

Historically, the way of negation speaks of God by saying what we cannot say.[19] "Negative theology," wrote Nicholas of Cusa (1401-1464), "is so indispensable to an affirmative theology that without it theology would be adored, not as the Infinite but rather as a creature, which is idolatry, or giving to an image what is due to Truth alone. . . . Sacred ignorance has taught us that God is ineffable, because He is infinitely greater than anything that words can express."[20]

Thus, talking about God in terms of what we cannot say leads finally to affirmation. To look on life and to see that there is "nowhere without No" is to find oneself uttering an ultimate yes. The next to the last word is that there is no final no. The last word is that there is only *yes* (II Corinthians 1:20)!

The great German mystic Jakob Böhme (1575-1624) said that "God is called the seeing and finding of the Nothing. And it is therefore called a Nothing (though it is God Himself) because it is inconceivable and inexpressible." To seek and to find "Nothing" means to seek and to find no thing or, in truth, all.

CHRISTIANITY FOR PIOUS SKEPTICS

In other words, in seeing and sensing, even when we only stammer, we stand on the threshold of recognition. Within us lies "an innate affinity for making contact with reality."[21] *That in which we dwell* comes to us from outside, *from beyond*. It is wholly other, beyond our imagining and apart from our intending. It is no thing and, therefore, all. *That of which we speak* appears to us as from inside, *from within*. It is from us, within our consciousness and a part of our mastery. It is every thing and, therefore, all.

Nicholas of Cusa insisted that God is seen only "beyond the coincidence of contradictories . . . and nowhere this side thereof." In other words, God is not one of the poles of any pair of contrasts.[22] "The opposition of opposites," contended Nicholas, "is an opposition without opposition." God can neither be reduced to a left-hemisphere intention nor contained in the in-touch awareness of the right hemisphere. As Augustine confessed to God: "Neither art thou the mind itself. For thou art the Lord God of the mind." Thus, Clement could rightly speak of this reality as "the Depth" because it contains and fosters all things, "inaccessible and boundless."

Tillich termed this "the God above the God of theism."[23] In the God above God we avoid "the loss of [ourselves] by participation." The I-consciousness of the left hemisphere depends upon the indwelling quality of the right. Likewise, in the God above God we avoid "the loss of our world by individualization." The am-awareness of the right hemisphere depends upon left-hemisphere intentionality.

We can and must speak of God. Yet we can never speak properly. No matter how much we say, we cannot say enough. No matter how little we talk, we still talk too much. Whether we speak up or remain silent, both count for naught.

Of all who have talked of God, perhaps none has spoken more comprehensively than the Italian philosopher Thomas Aquinas (1225?–1274). Based upon Aristotelean logic (left hemisphere) and inspired by Christian vision (right hemisphere), he spoke always and ever of God.

Toward the end of his life Aquinas became increasingly immersed in contemplation and ecstatic rapture. He finally gave up writing and speaking about God. When pressed to continue by his servant, he replied, "I cannot, Reginald, for everything that I have written appears to me . . . as so much rubbish compared with what I have seen, and what has been revealed to me!"[24]

Words fail in the presence of Presence!

In a post-critical faith we speak of God in ways that reduce nonsense and increase making sense. We are not content merely with what we take to be worthwhile; we seek that which is valid as well. We would acknowledge "the presence of something real and external to us."[25] It is not accidental that Augustine spoke of God as the "power which links together my mind with my inmost thoughts."

In talking of God we must know whereof we speak. Meaningful words depend upon real experience. What we say requires the empirical and the experiential.

Faith begins in an indwelling act of worship rather than as a statement of belief. As such, the indwelling quality of the right hemisphere precedes the intentionality of the left: Am before I!

At one point in his *Confessions*, Augustine declared: "Belatedly I loved thee [O Lord]: For see thou wast within and I without, and I sought thee out there."[26]

In speaking of God, we find we are brought to ourselves. We face what is inside, not what is outside. God is, with Augustine, more inward than our most inward part and higher than our highest reach. Our attention shifts from argument to experience. Within, behind, and beyond our words stands the Word.[27]

If using the Bible led us to speak of God, speaking of God brings us to praying for the Spirit.

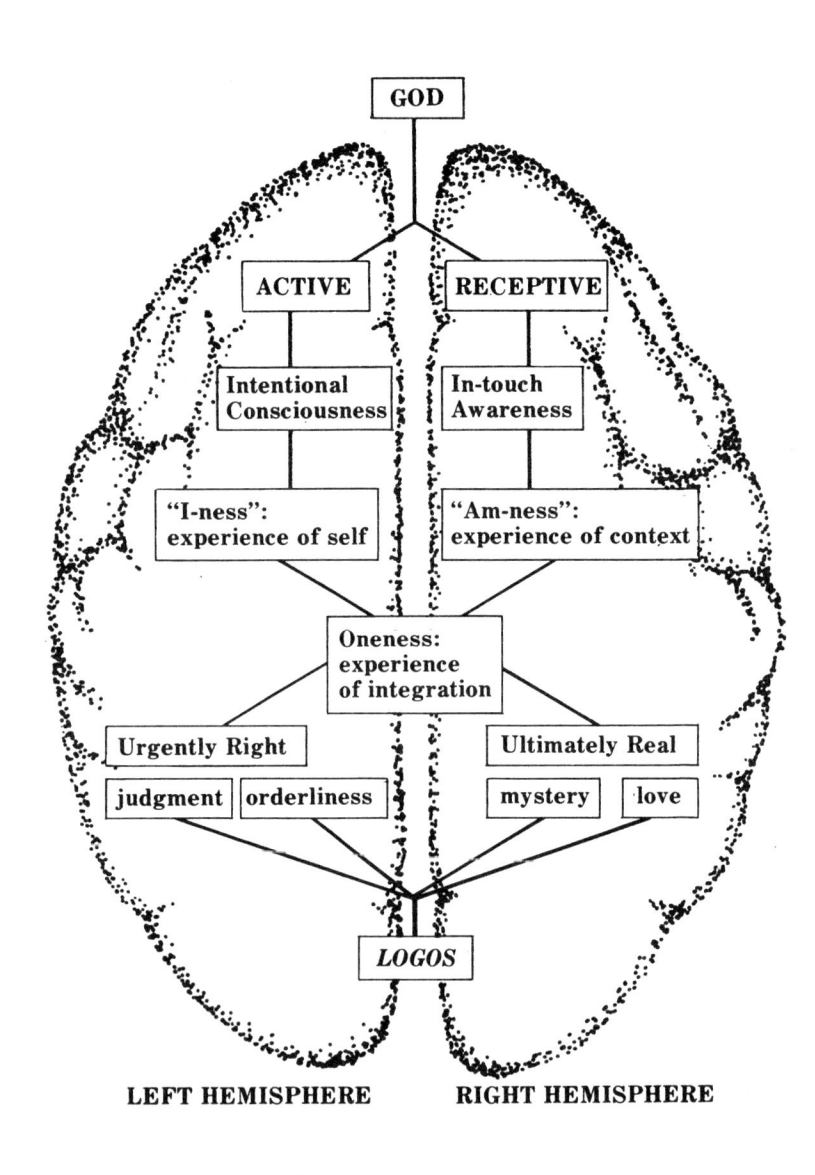

```
                    ┌─────┐
                    │ GOD │
                    └──┬──┘
            ┌──────────┴──────────┐
      ┌─────┴──────┐       ┌──────┴─────┐
      │  ACTIVE    │       │ RECEPTIVE  │
      └─────┬──────┘       └──────┬─────┘
      ┌─────┴──────┐       ┌──────┴─────┐
      │ Intentional│       │  In-touch  │
      │Consciousness│      │ Awareness  │
      └─────┬──────┘       └──────┬─────┘
      ┌─────┴──────┐       ┌──────┴──────┐
      │ "I-ness":  │       │ "Am-ness":  │
      │experience  │       │ experience  │
      │ of self    │       │ of context  │
      └─────┬──────┘       └──────┬──────┘
            └──────────┬──────────┘
                 ┌─────┴──────┐
                 │  Oneness:  │
                 │ experience │
                 │of integration│
                 └─────┬──────┘
      ┌────────────────┴────────────────┐
┌─────┴──────┐                    ┌─────┴──────┐
│Urgently Right│                  │Ultimately Real│
└─────┬──────┘                    └─────┬──────┘
┌─────┴──┬──────────┐         ┌─────────┬─────┴──┐
│judgment│orderliness│        │ mystery │  love  │
└────────┴──────────┘         └─────────┴────────┘
            └──────────┬──────────┘
                 ┌─────┴──────┐
                 │   *LOGOS*  │
                 └────────────┘
```

LEFT HEMISPHERE　　　　**RIGHT HEMISPHERE**

IV. Praying for the Spirit: Receptive and Active

In speaking of religious experience, William James spoke of "the little more and how much it is, and the little less and what worlds away!"[1] It is that "little less" and "what worlds away" that so characterizes reasonable religion. In thinking more people find they are feeling less.

Surprisingly, the late 1960s and early 1970s have erupted with a third Great Awakening in America. It is not unlike the 1730s in New England and the 1820s in New York and Ohio. The current awakening has both secular and religious eruptions. People are looking not for definitions but, as Martin Marty observes, "for immediacy," not for explanations but, as Andrew Greeley reports, for "illumination." There is a shift from self-sufficiency to seeking.[2]

Thus, it is not surprising that the little i's of the immediate, the intimate, the intense, the imaginative, and the inspiring are matched by the big m's of myth, mystery, mysticism, meditation, and meaning.[3] From having sold our minds for too many words, we are longing to recover our souls in wordless wonder. An old Zen saying has it "better to see the face than to hear the name." Isaiah prayed: "O that thou wouldst rend the heavens and come down" (Isaiah 64:1).

Post-critical faith directs us to rediscover experience. We must move from a too intense doing to a more attentive being. But how? Again, the one brain with two hemispheres provides a model. We are to shift from left-hemisphere domination to right-hemisphere discovery. Let me explain.

Passive Reception

Initially, activating the right hemisphere involves a passivity, a letting go of conscious activity to allow free-floating awareness. We stop thinking. We stop talking. We stop staring. We simply let be.

In depicting the Ascent of the Mount of Perfection, St. John of the Cross gave directions for quieting the left hemisphere and activating the right:

> If you want to know all,
>   You must desire to know nothing.
> If you want to arrive at that which you know not,
>   You must go by a way which you know not.
> If you want to arrive at that which you possess not,
>   You must go by a way which you possess not.
> If you want to arrive at that which you are not,
>   You must pass through that which you are not.

"In this nakedness," St. John went on, "the spiritual soul finds its quietude and rest; since it covets nothing, nothing wearies it in its upward flight, and nothing oppresses it when it is cast down; for the soul then abides in the center of its humility."[4]

I know no more penetrating description of receptivity than that. Here is the basis of praying for the Spirit.

External Stimuli

At the very least, we open ourselves to the visual, the sensory, the wordless: music and melody and movement.

No logic, only longing, passively taking in whatever is presented.

When we observe experience intellectually, we erect a screen, as it were, between ourselves and what we see. We remain apart. In contrast, as Michael Polanyi pointed out, in contemplation we dissolve the screen, stop our movement through experience, and thus, pour ourselves straight into experience.[5]

Karl Barth reported that for years he played Mozart each morning before working on his *Dogmatics*. Thomas Merton suggests that "unconsciously [Barth was] seeking to awaken, perhaps the hidden sophianic Mozart in himself, the central wisdom that comes in tune with the divine and cosmic music and is saved by love, yes, even by *eros*. While the other, theological self [what I identify as the rational left hemisphere], seemingly more concerned with love, grasps at a more stern, more cerebral *agape*: a love that, after all, is not in our own heart but *only in God* and revealed only to our head. Barth says," Merton goes on, that "it is a child, even a 'divine' child, who speaks in Mozart's music to us."[6]

Contemplation of nature parallels such contemplation of music. One feels renewed in the pink and blue of a morning sky, the yellow and red of a setting sun, or the lush green of a wooded grove. Chinese landscape painting is unsurpassed in its expression of such contemplation. Since orderliness and harmony (*Li*) pervade all nature, all nature is deserving of attentiveness. By emptying the mind of distractions, artists found the universe surrendering to them. In that meeting they discerned meaning.

Devotional reading also falls within the area of receptiveness to external stimuli. Here one gives oneself to ideas and images on the page. The material itself is regarded as special or sacred—that is, worth immersing oneself in. We take in uncritically in order to be illumined and enlivened.

Landscape: Scenery with Distant Mountains
—Lu Chih (sixteenth century)

Courtesy of the Art Institute of Chicago
H. W. Mead Fund Purchase

In using the Bible, Martin Luther told people to listen "to the Word coming from the book and to the echo" in themselves.[7] The Word reduces prejudice; the echo encourages presence. Perhaps that receptivity is what John Calvin meant by the Bible being our authority "only when the divine spirit witnesses to it (the *testimonium Sancti Spiritus internum*)."[8] When the inner witness is lacking, the Bible has little meaning.

Internal Stimuli

More than responding to music or nature or words, however, the receptivity to which I point touches on the Quaker practice of waiting for the Inner Light. For the Quakers, inspiration and insight rise up and direct thought if given an opportunity.

Jakob Böhme's advice to a novice in the spiritual search applies to the practice of receptiveness to internal stimuli:

> When both thy intellect and will are quiet and passive to the expressions of the eternal Word and Spirit . . . *then* the eternal Hearing, Seeing, and Speaking will be revealed in thee. Blessed art thou therefore if thou canst stand still from self thinking and self willing and canst stop the wheel of thy imagination and senses.[9]

We are to respond below the level of conscious intention. More than simply letting things happen, we practice presence.

Active Participation

In practicing presence we shift from passive reception into active participation. We disengage from the ordinary. Less stimuli bombard us. We block out sights and sounds. Increasingly, we find what Sören Kierkegaard spoke of as purity of heart—doing one thing, willing the will of God. Simultaneously, there are experiences of loss and experiences of gain.[10] We lose a sense of time and place, of limitations and desires, of thoughts and sensory awareness. We gain a sense of timelessness and unity, of release and new life, of identification and ineffability.

Basic procedures help us stop trying and let be.[11] We locate a quiet place with a set time where we go apart to enter into "the closet" (Matthew 6:6). We deeply relax our body from feet to face to wait upon the Spirit (Isaiah 40:31). We find an object upon which to focus. It could be a cross, an image such as Jesus, a phrase such as "love," or a procedure such as counting one's breath. We get in a comfortable position that allows us to remain relaxed but alert (Mark 14:37-38). Regardless of particulars the effects are the same: we reduce left-hemisphere activity and bodily arousal.[12]

Such active participation in letting go includes letting go of ideas and words. Here we use our imagination to move into images that rise up from the unconscious or that move in from the edges of awareness. We attend to them yet let them be a continuous flow. Within the pieces lies our peace. The integrating Spirit, the "inner physician" as Augustine called it, works to reconcile that which has been torn apart. There comes a healing of the hurt in the heart and a soothing of the ache in the head.

Such imaginative immersion in the twilight zone of consciousness assumes, from a theological point of view, the omnipresence of God. The psalmist expresses that negatively when he writes: There is no place to escape from Spirit, for "both dark and light are one" (Psalm 139:12 NEB). Late classical mysticism expressed this concept positively when it declared that everything spiritual has a lower and higher meaning.[13]

Whether omnipresence is experienced as grace or as

judgment, we participate actively in receiving what is presented from beyond the sensory and within the reasonable. We open ourselves to the future with its surprising power and discover ourselves responding affirmatively to what is and to what is to be.

Procedures

Uncritical warmth admonishes us to pray, yet seldom provides reasonable means for praying. Critical coolness avoids prayer yet finds no replacement for receptivity. A new alliance, a reunion of openness and reasonableness, is called for.

Meditation

For me, there is no substitute for meditating—not reading, not thinking, not talking, not encountering, not acting. While each of these has value, none opens the deeper dimension of Otherness. We are to shape the environment around us in order to activate the world within us, in activating the world within us we awaken the world beyond us. In meditation we wait and wait and wait, without ideas, without images, without expectations. We wait in the pregnant void for the birth of a presence beyond anything we can ask or imagine.

We begin meditating by becoming actively inactive, alert but not aroused, receptive without responding. Too many ideas and too many words get in the way. Ideas and words keep the left hemisphere active and cut off the energy of the right hemisphere.

In meditation we practice simple, centered awareness, a giving up of self-consciousness, a cultivation of simple surrender.

Most meditative practices involve a twofold effort.[14]

1. We cultivate an inner silence, a temporary stopping of ego-controlled activity. These usually involve differentiating, distinguishing, categorizing, judging, evaluating.
2. We seek a state of receptiveness to aspects of reality that are subtle in that they do not fit easily or readily into preestablished mind-sets.

Both the cultivation of inner silence and the discovery of the subtle allow us to step out of the way so that our deeper selfhood may emerge.

Listening to music, looking at nature, or reading devotional literature is not enough. What more is needed? Silence, solitude, surrender. "It is really a silent surrendering of everything to God," wrote Kierkegaard, "because it is not quite plain to me how I should pray."

Early in meditative practice we avoid content. One person called this procedure a spring housecleaning of the mind.[15] Mystic Richard St. Victor declared: Forget. Forget. Forget. St. John of the Cross admonished: Nothing. Nothing. Nothing.[16]

Nothing has influenced meditation more than emphasis on breathing. Breath is the foundation of life. To follow our breathing is to enter into that realm into which and through which and from which all reality flows. We put ourselves below and beyond words. Whatever else, breathing prepares the way for what is real. Breath connects us to life and prepares the way for deeper unification.[17] As Jesus breathed upon his disciples, they received the Spirit (John 20:22).

Meditation is a way of doing one thing at a time all the time. Lawrence LeShan describes it as an activity by which we seek to find, recover, and "come back to something of ourselves we once dimly and unknowingly had and have lost without knowing what it was or when we lost it."[18] The goal is "the fullest use of what it means to be human." Two consequences follow: (1) greater efficiency in everyday life by virtue of "learning to do one thing at a time," and (2) comprehension of another view of reality than the sensory, temporal, spatial, causal reality of the observable.

Regardless of approach, breath-counting is basic. One gets as comfortable as possible, with as few distractions as possible, and simply follows one's breath, letting it set its own pace and depth. Hard as that is, one attends solely to breathing. In a few minutes breathing slows down. There is a general quieting of the entire body.

Once one has had experience attending to breathing, one begins counting breaths. At first, count one on inhaling and two in exhaling. After a while, count one on exhaling, inhale, and count two on exhaling, and so on. One may count from one to four and begin again, or count from one to ten and begin again. Many people become lost around five or six and, therefore, four may be easier. To count only to one—which is what Zen master Nanrei Kobori recommended to me for Westerners who are in a hurry to get enlightenment—seems too rigorous.

Meditative approaches vary in their use of that freer, slower, deeper breathing.[19] There are three distinct ways.

There is the Way of Forms: objects or symbols to which one attends. Practices are directive, concentrative, absorptive. One places oneself under the influence of the focal point as a single, unchanging stimulus. In effect, the Way of Forms tells us: "Here is truth, assimilate it."

In the Expressive Way, practices are nondirective, expansive, spontaneous. One is guided by whatever promptings prompt. One surrenders to the spontaneous and the unexpected. In effect, the Expressive Way instructs us: "Truth lies within, and you find it by forgetting ready-made answers."

There is a third or Negative Middle Way. In this,

practices detach one from everything through elimination and emptying. One moves away from objects, ideas, and images by not staying with anything that one perceives. In effect, the Negative Middle Way announces: "Let go of preference and preconception; simply mirror what is without adding to or taking away; stay with bare attention."

In meditation we recover contact with ourselves and with the wholeness of the universe. We are at one!

Prayer

If we begin by getting rid of words, we end by putting into words. Despite his own ecstatic experience, the apostle Paul informs us that we are to pray with the spirit *(pneumati)* and with understanding *(noi)* (I Corinthians 14:15). In my model of the brain, that means we pray both with the receptive right hemisphere and with the active left hemisphere. We are to take in, and we are to give out. We attend and we intend. In truth, we intend to attend! In fact, we attend to intend!

Meditation and prayer are not ends in themselves. They are means to the end of God's being all in all. To turn inward in order to turn on can never be an escape from the ongoing. In starting with ourselves, which is what meditation demands, we discover we end with the all, making contact with the way things are. What "begins in mysticism . . . ends in politics."[20]

The vision of reality is not simply the joy of our being at home in the universe. That vision is inclusive, requiring that everyone and everything be at home. Meister Eckhart (1260?-1327) expressed it precisely: "What we have gathered in contemplation we give out in love."

The borders between self and environment disappear.[21] The self actually embraces others. "Self-consciousness becomes social consciousness." The same applies to the physical environment—the rape of nature literally becomes the destruction of self.

To open ourselves to receiving the way things really are is to have to take in "the maximum amount of the problematic of life."[22] In the end, to pray for the Spirit returns us to the sensory realm. From forgetting ourselves by being beside ourselves, we are mobilized for more than ourselves. Instead of being anxious about many things, now we are caught up in whatever is necessary.

At the conclusion of my meditating, I ask what I have sought: I pray, "O Lord, receive me that I can receive thee. And in receiving thee I can receive all. In receiving all I would respond to all, even though I am changed."

The soul of otherness lies embedded in the substance of "this-ness." Personal prayer carries within it prophetic mysticism. In seeing what is real, we are confronted with what is right. To be turned on results in being turned around *(metanoia)*. Expanded consciousness leads to decisive commitment.

To pray for the Spirit brings us to the call of Christ. We are to live for him!

Movement

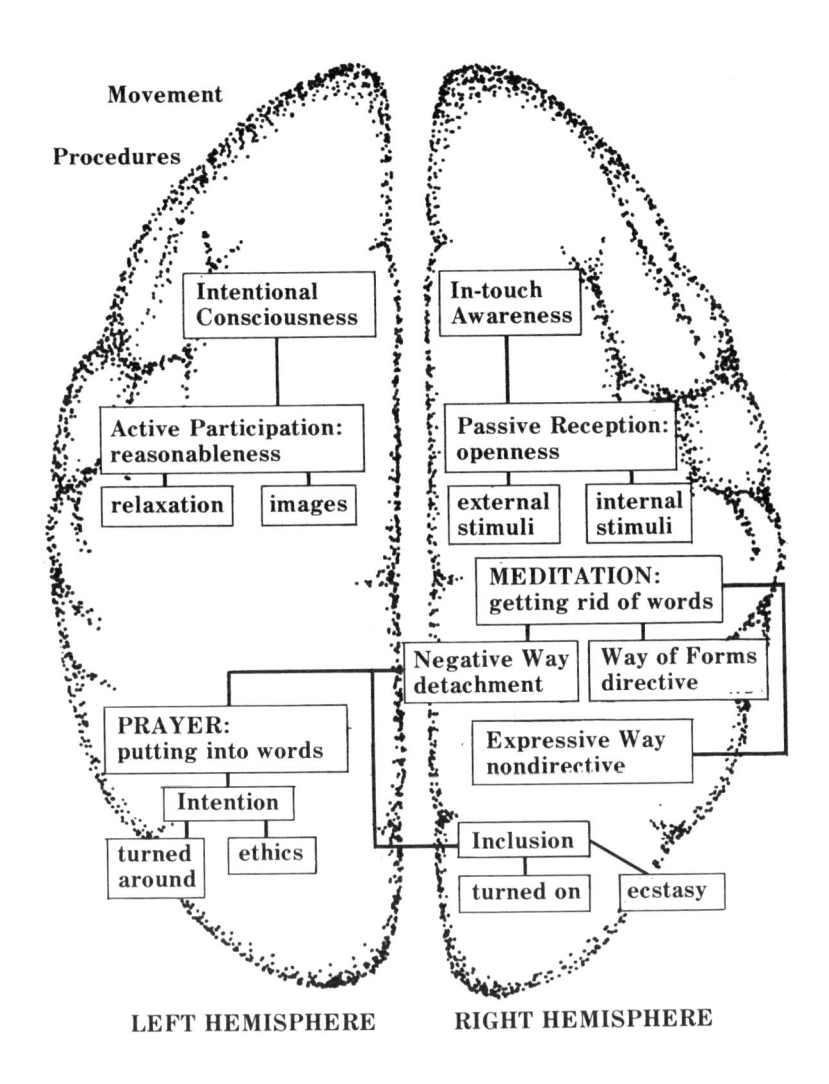

Procedures

Intentional Consciousness

Active Participation: reasonableness

relaxation | images

In-touch Awareness

Passive Reception: openness

external stimuli | internal stimuli

MEDITATION: getting rid of words

Negative Way detachment | Way of Forms directive

Expressive Way nondirective

PRAYER: putting into words

Intention

turned around | ethics

Inclusion

turned on | ecstasy

LEFT HEMISPHERE   **RIGHT HEMISPHERE**

V. Living for Christ: Limits and Affirmations

The receptive right hemisphere roots us in the mysticism of eternity. The active left hemisphere thrusts us into a prophetic engagement in history. E. B. White expressed the dilemma of this prophetic mysticism:

> If the world were merely seductive, that would be easy. If it were merely challenging, that would be no problem, but I arise in the morning torn between a desire to improve [or save] the world and a desire to enjoy [or savor] the world. This makes it hard to plan the day.[1]

Saving or savoring, improving or enjoying, the active left or the receptive right? These contrasts drive us to seek an integrating whole: one brain with two hemispheres, one mind with two mind-sets, one universe with two realms—interconnected, interpenetrating, interdependent. All saving requires savoring and all savoring necessitates saving.

In the event of the Incarnation—the Word becoming flesh and dwelling among us—the contrasting patterns are brought together, even as they are distinguishable. In Jesus as the Christ, we are confronted by two faces of one reality. Here is the event that illumines all events (John 1:4-5)!

In him we see divinity. Through interpreting the history of Jesus as the Christ we understand the history of humanity. Because of that we stand receptively in the midst of life taking in what is, as it is, without addition or subtraction at each and every level (the physical, the psychic, the spiritual), which means taking in life in love.

Through Christ we shape humanity. We act with clarity, initiating what is to become, as it is to become, without distraction or desertion at each and every level (the physical, the psychic, the spiritual), which means giving out in love.

A post-critical faith leads us to ask: What do we see when we see life in him? How do we act when we shape life through him?

The Limit-Setting of Light

First I see and hear a *no*—a lightning flash of limitation.

Against Withdrawal

His *no* stands against a timeless ecstasy that withdraws from this world into an other-worldly asceticism.

In the economy of God's kingdom there is no space for those who pray and never picket; for those who meditate and never mediate; for those who look to the throne of grace and never see the outcast, the downtrodden, the sick, the imprisoned, the halt and the lame, the blind and the deaf, the destitute and the deserted, the world with all its warts and all its worries, people with all their pain and all their perplexities.

In the ecstatic mind-set we would build temples and stay put. We would remain on the mountaintop of transfiguration (Mark 9:5). To such a longing, Christ says: "No! Return! Be about the business of humanizing! Proclaim liberation! Seek transformation for all!"

Against Embeddedness

Christ also stands against a too grim existence that immerses itself in worldly materialism.

In the politics of God's kingdom there is no time for those who do and never are, for those who run and never rest, for those who bristle and never bend, for those who shout and never listen, for those who look to the balance sheets and bargain tables of food and clothes and shelter and security.

In the mind-set of the everyday we would build houses and hurry on (Luke 12:16-21). We are about the business of building the Kingdom on our own for ourselves. To such a busyness, Christ always says: "No! Turn aside! Stop what you are doing! You are harried and anxious about many things! One thing alone is needed—genuine presence!"

In interpreting life through the light of Jesus as the Christ I see this clear *no*. He stands against a spiritualism that sets living off in special space—sterilized and purified, a timeless realm of ecstasy and mystery. He reminds us that the farther reaches of humanity must never distract us from the nearer ravages of inhumanity.

He stands against a materialism that presses life into special time—anxious and stressful, a spaceless realm of activity and mastery. He reminds us that the nearer ravages of inhumanity must never divert us from the farther reaches of humanity.

As crucified divinity and resurrected humanity, Christ Jesus neither glorifies this world nor another. He rejects an easy accommodation here and now by setting loose "powers that are critical of being." He dismisses a glorified ecstasy there and then "by pressing forwards to the future of a new reality." The issue is transformed reality here and now![2]

The Affirmation of Life

Even as I hear Christ's no, so I hear his *yes*. That affirmation is spectacular and awesome, lighting up history's horizon.

For Everyone

His *yes* declares that there are no more distinctions—neither male nor female, neither slave nor free, neither ins nor outs, neither rich nor poor, neither educated nor uneducated (Galatians 3:28).

> Christ is our living peace. He has made a unity of the conflicting elements of Jew and Gentile by breaking down the dividing wall of hostility . . . so as to create out of the two a single new humanity in himself, thereby making peace (Ephesians 2:11-16, author's paraphrase).

In the economy of God's kingdom there are no longer first-class citizens with first-class seats and second-class citizens with second-class seats. In God's kingdom there are no longer those with authority and those without authority. There are no longer top dogs and underdogs. In Christ Jesus all are one—yes, one, without distinction—for we are all children of God.

For Everything

Christ's *yes* equally discloses that there are no more divisions either in nature or history: nothing is so distinctive as to be decisive, and nothing so ordinary as to be irrelevant. No longer is there a dualism—a divorce—a dividing wall of hostility—between this sphere and that sphere, between this space and that space.

In the politics of God's kingdom there is no sacred and secular, religious and nonreligious, spiritual and material. Christ has entered into every place and embraced every part. By his presence he has hallowed everything—yes, he has become all in all, ever present, everywhere (Colossians 3:10-11), world without end, amen: no divisions, for the kingdoms of this world are, in truth, the kingdom of our Lord and of his Christ (Revelation 11:15).

The incarnation presents us with a clarity that encompasses everything and everyone. In him the *no* of prophetic protests meets the *yes* of mystical participation. All are one and One is all.

Nicholas of Cusa contended that in God "centre and circumference are one . . . and in Him at the right moment the centre-seeking body and the circumference-tending soul shall be united."[3]

In Jesus as the Christ—the showing forth of the Logos, the ordering and orderly structure of the universe—we see that convergence of body and soul, of center-seeking and circumference-tending, of making whole and making holy.

Because of the crucified clarifier we long for the liberation of all. Both reason and passion are subjected to an ethical demand; love be manifested through justice and justice be transformed by love. We declare as needed and necessary the full potential of everyone and everything. More important than hidden wholeness is future wholeness.

In the crucified clarifier we see more than is at present apparent. Within the aching void we sense a fullness waiting to be born. We are surprised at the fresh ways in which the future comes in both its oddness and its ordinariness.

Undoubtedly, there is truth in the old saying that in taking the first sip from the beaker of knowledge we are separated from God. Nevertheless, those who keep drinking—seeking ultimate and urgent reality—discover God waiting for them at the bottom of the beaker.[4]

An Intentional Life-Style

Even as we say something because of the crucified Jesus, so we see life because of the risen Christ.

In living for Christ, post-critical wholeness includes yet

```
                    the mind
                    of God
                       |
                    the mind
                    of Christ
                       |
                    the human mind
                       |
                    intentionality
         /         /         \         \
    no          no           for         for
 embeddedness  withdrawal   everything  everyone
         \       /             \       /
          NO:                   YES:
       limit-setting          affirmation
              \                 /
                   CHRIST

         LEFT           RIGHT
      HEMISPHERE     HEMISPHERE
```

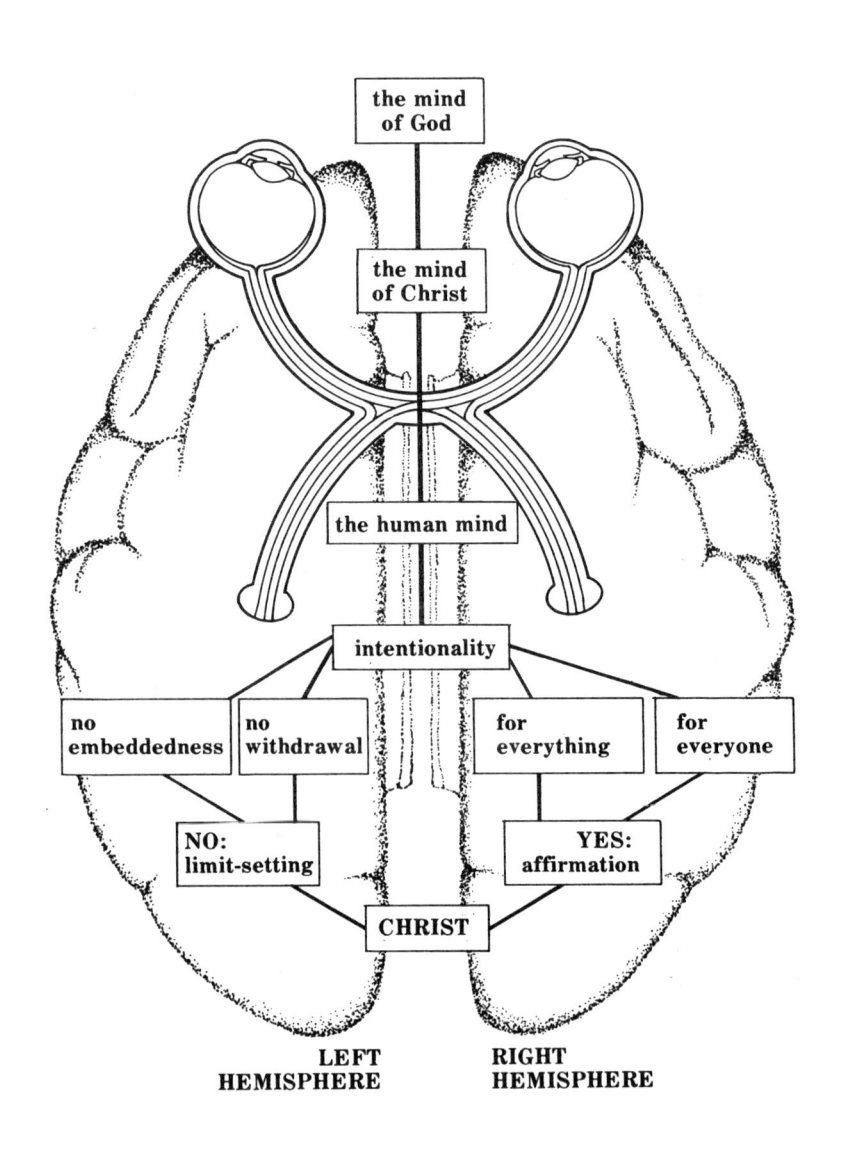

transcends the analytical. We recall the paradigm of one brain with two hemispheres. The critical, articulate left hemisphere combines with the relational, creative right hemisphere for an intentional Christianity. We deliberate, decide, and determine our style of life and our stake in the world. We attend to how we are to be. We intend what we are to do. We choose to take upon ourselves the burden and possibility of wholeness. As all things cohere in Christ, so we are to hold all things together in ourselves (Colossians 1:17, 28).

We cultivate the inner life of the Spirit—contemplating, meditating, praying, listening, waiting, taking in the larger life of which we are a part and in which we participate.

We cultivate the intimate life of love—caring, being cared for, disclosing, distributing grace and growth among those close to us.

We cultivate the outer life of justice—liberating every person and every sphere to become full-grown and mature, realizing all that is meant to be.

In getting ourselves together we actually intend to give ourselves away.[5] In giving ourselves away—dying for Christ—we discover we have gotten ourselves together. Life is larger, even though it may not be easier. In Christ, writes John MacQuarrie, "the full openness of God and the potential openness of (humanity) have converged. . . . What is ambiguous and obscured in everyday human existing is revealed and manifested in the Christ. Here is an openness to the world, openness to the neighbor, the manifestation of God's openness in the flesh . . . 'incarnation.'"[6]

In living for Christ nothing is precluded; everything is included. "Everything belongs to you!" writes Paul to the Corinthians, "the world, life, death, the present or the future, everything is yours!" Without exception all is ours. "For you belong to Christ, and Christ belongs to God" (I Corinthians 3:21-23 Phillips).

We intend to take in, to be part of, to act with and to press on in every sphere.

In Jesus as the Christ—the incarnate presence of indwelling power—that center-seeking body—we experience convergence, a coming together, of all humanity in the family of life.

In Jesus as the Christ—the incarnate presence of intentional purpose—that circumference-tending soul—we experience divergence, a going forth, of all humanity to the farthest reaches of the universe.

The "Mind" of Christ

Neither the mystery of nature nor the mastery of history contains the embodied life of what Paul Hammer terms "the whole-making Spirit." "The whole creation," declares the apostle Paul, "waits on tiptoe with eager longing for the revealing of humans as humans. The world of creation cannot as yet see reality because it has been so limited. The whole creation has been groaning in all its parts in a sort of universal travail, and not only the creation, but we ourselves are in a state of painful tension, groaning inwardly, while we wait for God to make us his and to realize our full identity in him" (Romans 8:19-23, author's paraphrase).

But, who knows the mind of God? No one! Instead, we are given "the mind of Christ" (I Corinthians 2:16).

The doctrine of the Incarnation rejects a divine essence without content. As the "light of the world," Christ presents us with the convergence of "the full openness of God and the potential openness of [humankind]." We see "the clue to the cosmos," as Robert McAfee Brown put it, "the picture in the empty picture frame."[7]

We are to have that mind—the one brain with its left and right hemispheres—"which was also in Christ" (Philippians). Here Paul calls us to the mind-set of Christ. We are to have the understanding, the feeling, the thinking, the intuiting, the intending, that were his.

Origen, and later Bernard of Clairvaux, spoke of the mystical marriage of the Logos and the soul. We are to intend that union—the mind of Christ—in us and among us. That is what the word "mind"—in Greek *proneo*—means. We are to have the disposition to transform simple feeling into mature compassion and simple thinking into mature wisdom. We are to have that ever-deepening and expanding consciousness that was in Christ.

As Jakob Böhme contended, it is the issue of Christ *in* us rather than Christ *for* us.[8] In giving up his own being, Christ lets us "be" by helping us become. As living center, he "gives reality to our analogies and assures us that they are not merely fanciful."[9]

The mind-set of Christ is easy yet impossible. It is impossible because we seldom know who he is or where he is. Like Mary Magdalene, we retreat to a garden of contemplation, thinking that by waiting in the quietness, away from the mastery of the sensory realm, we will find him. He still comes to us as a gardener. We look and see him not. We talk and hear him not. We reach out and touch him not (John 20:11-16).

Or, like the two on the road to Emmaus, we move with the traffic of the times, believing that in the battering of the marketplace, away from the mystery of the nonsensory realm, we will encounter him. He still comes to us as a stranger. We look and see him not. We talk and hear him not. We reach out and touch him not (Luke 24:13-24).

It is impossible to know who he is or where to find him. As gardener, he tells our receptive right hemisphere, "Go forth! Seek me not where all is still but where all is stirring!" As stranger, he tells our active left hemisphere, "Come apart! Seek me not where all is agitated but where all is leisurely." He is never where we think he is. He is ever where we suspect him least.

Nevertheless, the mind-set of Christ turns out to be the easiest task of all. For he is ever present, everywhere, in every way. Some of the time we know we are with him. Much of the time we wonder if we are. Yet all of the time we can live for him. We are to "take simple experience and connect it somehow to 'all things' that 'were created through Christ and for him'."[10] To live for Christ is to be alive to all—a new people in a new creation (II Corinthians 5).

The New Testament's conviction of the indwelling Spirit allows us to believe that we, too, can encounter God as ultimate and urgent reality "without intermediary." This "spark of the soul" (Meister Eckhart), this "ground" (John Tauler, ca. 1300-1361), this Inward Light (the Quakers), this "wonder of wonders," which is "great enough to be God, small enough to be me," is the immediate presence of all that is. "If," said Jakob Böhme, "thou conceivest a small minute circle, as small as a grain of mustard seed, yet the Heart of God, then there is in thyself (in the circle of thy life) the whole Heart of God undivided."[11]

A former student wrote a song that went like this:

> I'm walking to a new beat
> (Down the same street with the same feet)
> walking to a new beat

That is what post-critical faith is about: walking down the same street, with the same feet, but walking to a new beat.

We arrive where we started, not going in circles but spiraling with sophisticated simplicity.

We receive the wonders of God's world.

We act to make known the wondrous work of God!

We live beyond piety and skepticism!

NOTES

Chapter I
Dilemma and Direction

1. See Michael Polanyi, *Personal Knowledge: Towards a Post-Critical Philosophy* (Torchbooks; New York: Harper & Row, [1958] 1964), pp. 271-72.
2. Ian Barbour, *Myths, Models and Paradigms: A Comparative Study in Science and Religion* (New York: Harper, 1974).
3. A. R. Luria, "The Functional Organization of the Brain," *Scientific American*, March, 1970, pp. 66-78; Doreen Kimura, "The Asymmetry of the Human Brain," *Ibid.*, March, 1973, pp. 70-78; R. W. Sperry, "Hemisphere Disconnection and Unity of Conscious Awareness," *American Psychologist*, October, 1968, pp. 723-33.
4. If a photograph of a scene in nature is reversed as a mirror image, it is virtually impossible to recognize. If a photograph of a highway or street with signs is reversed, the change is immediately obvious. Michael C. Corballis and Ivan L. Beal, "On Telling Left from Right," in *Altered States of Awareness: Readings from "Scientific American,"* (San Francisco: W. H. Freeman, 1972), pp. 65-73.
5. The dominant lateralization of the left hemisphere applies to 13 out of 14 people who are right-handed. Little is known about left-handed persons. Some of them have their speech areas in the right hemisphere, but most have their speech areas in the left. Nigel Calder, *The Mind of Man: An Investigation into Current Research on the Brain and Human Nature* (New York: Viking Press, 1973), p. 248.

   Recent studies show slightly more than 1/3 of the population with marked left-hemisphere dominance and the rest with some left-hemisphere dominance. One out of 10 have a total absence of left-hemisphere dominance. A. R. Luria, *The Working Brain: An Introduction to Neuro-Psychology*, trans. Basil Haigh (New York: Basic Books, 1973), pp. 78-79.
6. Norman Geschwind, "Language and the Brain," *Scientific American*, April, 1972, pp. 76-83.
7. Robert E. Ornstein, *The Psychology of Consciousness* (San Francisco: W. H. Freeman, 1972). For more technical discussion see Robert E. Ornstein, ed., *The Nature of Human Consciousness: A Book of Readings* (San Francisco: W. H. Freeman, 1973).
8. Kimura, "Asymmetry of the Brain," pp. 73-74.
9. Geschwind, "Language and the Brain," p. 83.
10. *Ibid.*, p. 78.
11. J. C. Eccles, *Facing Reality: Philosophical Adventure by a Brain Scientist* (New York: Springer-Verlag, 1970), pp. 56, 73-80; R. W. Sperry, "The Great Cerebral Commissure," *Scientific American*, January, 1964, p. 46.

12. Luria, *Working Brain*, pp. 162-63.
13. Eccles, *Facing Reality*, p. 73.
14. Calder, *Mind of Man*, p. 252.
15. Sperry, "Cerebral Commissure," p. 49.
16. Lawrence LeShan, *The Medium, The Mystic and The Physicist: Toward a General Theory of the Paranormal* (New York: Viking Press, 1974), pp. 33-40, 86-87.
17. The interest and energy of younger evangelicals in social implications of the gospel suggests the radical shift in this position.

Chapter II

Using the Bible

1. G.W. Butterworth, ed., *Origen On First Principles* (Torchbooks; New York: Harper & Row, 1966), p. 288.
2. *Ibid.*, pp. xv-xvi.
3. Walter Wink, *The Bible in Human Transformation* (Philadelphia: Fortress Press, 1973).
4. Robert M. Grant, *A Short History of the Interpretation of the Bible*, rev. ed. (New York: Macmillan, 1963), p. 88.
5. In medieval times a system of allegorization developed. Four levels of meaning, and often as many as seven, were looked for in every text. For example, in Galatians 4, "Jerusalem" was understood (1) historically, as the city of the Jews, (2) allegorically, as the church of Christ, (3) anagogically (exemplifying spiritual interpretation), as the heavenly city that is the mother of all, and (4) morally, as the human soul. Grant, *Short History*, pp. 119-20.
6. Butterworth, *Origen*, pp. 275-76, 287-90, 294, 296-97, 312. Origen's "bodily meaning" meant interpretations made "by the simplest believers," those who could not grasp metaphors, parables, or allegories, who insisted on taking every detail literally. For them poetry was prose.
7. See J.E. Cirlot, *A Dictionary of Symbols*, 2d ed., trans. Jack Sage (New York: Philosophical Library, 1974), pp. 106-8. See also C. G. Jung, *Aion: Researches into the Phenomenology of the Self*, 2d ed., trans. R.F.C. Hull (London: Routledge & Kegan Paul, 1959), "The Sign of the Fishes," pp. 72-94; "The Ambivalence of the Fish Symbol," pp. 118-25; "The Fish in Alchemy," pp. 126-53; "The Alchemical Interpretation of the Fish," pp. 154-72.
8. Paul Tillich, *The Courage To Be* (New Haven: Yale University Press, 1952), pp. 179-80; 40, 176.
9. James B. Ashbrook, *Be/come Community* (Valley Forge, Pa.: Judson Press, 1971), pp. 117-24.
10. The term "kenotic" comes from the Greek word *kenosis* meaning emptying or depletion. In patristic literature it was a synonym for the

Incarnation, expressing the condescension of the Son of God. In modern theology it is used more broadly to describe Christ's voluntarily giving up his divine qualities and submitting to the contingencies of human life. See *The Interpreter's Dictionary of the Bible*, 5 vols. (Nashville: Abingdon, 1962), vol. K-Q, p. 7.
11. Wink, *The Bible*, p. 13.
12. James B. Ashbrook, *Humanitas; Human Becoming and Being Human* (Nashville: Abingdon, 1973), pp. 107-16.
13. James B. Ashbrook, *The Old Me and A New i: An Exploration of Personal Identity* (Valley Forge, Pa.: Judson Press, 1974), pp. 59-71.
14. Wink, *The Bible*, pp. 54-58.

Chapter III

Speaking of God

1. Harvey Cox, *The Seduction of the Spirit: The Use and Misuse of People's Religion* (New York: Simon & Schuster, 1973), p. 153.
2. See Langdon Gilkey, *Naming the Whirlwind: The Renewal of God-Language* (Indianapolis: Bobbs-Merrill, 1969), pp. 107-228.
3. I have exaggerated the positions for the sake of emphasis and my need for symmetry and polarity.
4. Ian Ramsey, *Christian Empiricism*, ed. Jerry H. Gill (London: Sheldon Press, 1974), p. 62.
5. Polanyi, *Personal Knowledge*, p. 311.
6. Ramsey, *Christian Empiricism*, pp. 63-65.
7. Eccles, *Facing Reality*, p. 80.
8. Polanyi, *Personal Knowledge* and *The Tacit Dimension* (Anchor Books; Garden City, N.Y.: Doubleday & Co., 1967).
9. Eccles, *Facing Reality*, pp. 72-73, 161.
10. Polanyi, *Personal Knowledge*, pp. x, 64.
11. Ramsey, *Christian Empiricism*, pp. 66, 130.
12. Polanyi, *Personal Knowledge*, p. 309.
13. John MacQuarrie, *God-Talk: An Examination of the Language and Logic of Theology* (New York: Harper, 1967), pp. 63-75.
14. This section draws upon MacQuarrie, *God-Talk*, and Ian T. Ramsey, *Religious Language: An Empirical Placing of Theological Phrases* (New York: Macmillan, [1957] 1963).
15. Alfred North Whitehead, *The Aims of Education and Other Essays* (Mentor Books; New York: New American Library, [1929] 1964), p. 48.
16. Adapted from James Baldwin, *The Fire Next Time* (New York: Dial Press, 1963), p. 66.
17. Erich Fromm, *You Shall Be As Gods: A Radical Interpretation of the Old Testament and Its Tradition* (New York: Holt, Rinehart and Winston, 1966), p. 31.

18. John A. T. Robinson, *Exploration into God* (London: SCM Press, 1967), p. 57.
19. Clement put it precisely: "Reach somehow the conception of the Almighty, knowing not what He is, but what He is not." William Wilson, trans., and Alexander Roberts and James Donaldson, eds., *The Writings of the Fathers* (1869).
20. Nicholas Cusa, *Of Learned Ignorance*, trans. Germain Heron (New Haven: Yale University Press, 1954), pp. 59-60.
21. Polanyi, *Personal Knowledge*, p. 403.
22. Nicholas Cusa, *The Vision of God*, trans. Emma Gurney Salter, and intro. Evelyn Underhill (New York: Dutton, 1928), p. 44; Robinson, *Exploration into God*, pp. 139-40.
23. Tillich, *Courage To Be*.
24. Roger B. Vaughn, *The Life and Labours of S. Thomas Aquin* (London: Longmans Green, Ltd., 1872), pp. 913-19, 926.
25. Polanyi, *Personal Knowledge*, p. 202.
26. Augustine, *Confessions and Enchiridion*, ed. and trans. Albert C. Outler (Philadelphia: Westminster Press, 1955), Book III, 6:68.
27. Theology clarifies and corrects religious experience with its subsequent expression. By itself theology does not *and* cannot generate such experience.

Chapter IV
Praying for the Spirit

1. William James, *The Varieties of Religious Experience* (New York: Modern Library, 1902), p. 420.
2. Martin E. Marty, *The Fire We Can Light: The Role of Religion in a Suddenly Different World* (Garden City, N.Y.: Doubleday, 1973), pp. 54, 71-72; Andrew M. Greeley, *Ecstasy: A Way of Knowing* (Englewood Cliffs, N.J.: Prentice-Hall, 1974), p. 5.
3. Marty, *Fire We Can Light*, p. 175.
4. St. John of the Cross, *The Dark Night of the Soul*, ed. and trans. Kurt F. Reinhardt (New York: Frederick Ungar Publishing Co., 1957), pp. 26-27.
5. Polanyi, *Personal Knowledge*, p. 197.
6. Thomas Merton, *Conjectures of A Guilty Bystander* (Image Books; Garden City, N.Y.: Doubleday, [1966] 1968), pp. 11-12.
7. Erik H. Erikson, *Young Man Luther: A Study in Psychoanalysis and History* (New York: W.W. Norton, 1958), p. 210.
8. Paul Tillich, *Perspectives on Nineteenth and Twentieth Century Protestant Thought*, ed. Carl E. Braaten (New York: Harper, 1967), pp. 26-27.
9. Quoted in Evelyn Underhill, *Mysticism* (New York: Dutton, [1911] 1961), p. 64.
10. Margharita Laski, *Ecstasy* (Bloomington: Indiana University Press, 1967), pp. 130-31.

11. Herbert Benson, *The Relaxation Response* (New York: Morrow, 1975).
12. Robert Keith Wallace and Herbert Benson, "The Physiology of Meditation," in *Altered States of Awareness*, pp. 125-31.
13. Carl G. Jung, *Symbols of Transformation*, Vol. 1: *An Analysis of the Prelude to a Case of Schizophrenia*, trans. R.F.C. Hull (Torchbooks; New York: Harper & Row, [1956] 1962), p. 50.
14. Claudio Naranjo and Robert E. Ornstein, *On the Psychology of Meditation* (New York: Viking Press, 1971), p. 144.
15. Evelyn Underhill, *Practical Mysticism* (New York: Dutton, 1915), p. 19.
16. Cited in William Johnston, *The Still Point: Reflections on Zen and Christian Mysticism* (New York: Perennial Library, 1971), p. 31.
17. William Johnston, *Christian Zen* (New York: Harper, 1971), p. 79.
18. Lawrence Le Shan, *How to Meditate: A Guide to Self-Discovery* (Boston: Little Brown, 1974), pp. 4-5, 12-17.
19. See Naranjo and Ornstein, *Psychology of Meditation*.
20. Greeley, *Ecstasy*, p. 49; Peguy, quoted in Cox, *Seduction;* p. 189.
21. W.G. Roll, "Postscript: Psychical Research in Relation to Higher States of Consciousness." in *The Highest State of Consciousness*, ed. John White (Anchor Books, Garden City, N.Y.: Doubleday & Co., 1972), p. 471.
22. Ernest Becker, *The Denial of Death* (New York: The Free Press, 1973), p. 279.

Chapter V

Living for Christ

1. Matthew Fox, *On Becoming a Musical Mystical Bear: Spirituality American Style* (New York: Harper, 1972), p. 98.
2. "An eschatology of the cross [is] hostile to every eschatological ecstasy of fulfillment." Jurgen Moltmann, *Theology of Hope* (London: SCM Press, 1967), pp. 160-62, 68-69.
3. Cusa, *Of Learned Ignorance*, p. 117.
4. Aniela Jaffé, *The Myth of Meaning*, trans. R.F.C. Hull (New York: Putnam's, 1971), p. 36.
5. Ashbrook, *The Old Me*, pp. 85-105.
6. MacQuarrie, *God-Talk*, pp. 210-11.
7. Robert McAfee Brown, "From Clown to Fish: Contemporary Images of Jesus," *Christian Century*, February 23, 1972, p. 224.
8. John Joseph Stoudt, *Jacob Boehme: His Life and Thought* (New York: The Seabury Press, 1968), p. 51.
9. MacQuarrie, *God-Talk*, p. 227.
10. Marty, *Fire We Can Light*, p. 112.
11. Quoted in Underhill, *Mysticism*, pp. 100-101.

Epilogue:
Wholeness of Soul and Oneness with God

Like most people we search for glimpses of what matters. We do so because we believe we have been created and called by that which is really real. The anonymous fourteen-century author of *The Cloud of Unknowing* expressed this mystically when he linked wholeness of soul and oneness with God. In finding our own reality, we discover ultimate reality.

Our search has led us to recover basic and ancient truths:

faith and reason belong together;
life in the spirit and life in the body are interwoven;
ecstacy and ethics are inseparable.

Although we started at separate points, we discovered that our concerns led us toward a common path. Ashbrook's search moved from current understandings of the mind to persisting issues of religious faith. Walaskay's convictions led from past understandings of the heart to pressing concerns of contemporary reason. We found ourselves drawn together as pious skeptics in quest of a post-critical faith.

Fractured Faith

This book opened with the dream of the apostle Paul's beheading. The decapitation dramatizes, even as it symbolizes, the violation of our humanity, the severing of passion from reason. That split—be it physically, philosophically, or dogmatically induced—has wreaked havoc on humanity's being and becoming. Righteous indignation has often meant irrational fanaticism, while reasonable consideration has often led to passionless paralysis. The dream reminds us that in a fully functioning person, head and heart (and guts, too) must not be severed.

We also noted that an analogous severing of essential components can be seen in recent work with brain-injured people. Research has shown that our single head holds "two brains"—the right and left hemispheres of the cerebral cortex—and that each hemisphere specializes toward certain kinds of mental activity. The left hemisphere, which controls the right side of the body, is the center of logical and verbal activity; it "takes the puzzle apart." This hemisphere is also associated with control of the voluntary nervous system and, therefore, biological and individual survival.

The right hemisphere, which controls the left side of the body, seems to have a complementary function. It is the center of holistic and nonverbal mentation; it, in contrast, "puts the pieces together." This hemisphere is associated with control of the autonomic nervous sytem—the unresisting, passive monitoring of our pulmonary-cardiac system and, therefore, communal and psychic survival.

In active volition we tense the body, brace ourselves, tighten up to meet a challenge. There is intentional consciousness. In passive volition we relax the body, detach ourselves, let go of effort to simply be part of what is. Here is in-touch awareness.

In our exploration of pious skepticism we began with the image of the execution of Paul and moved to the more precise model of the split brain. Body and head in the first instance, and right and left hemisphere in the second, have

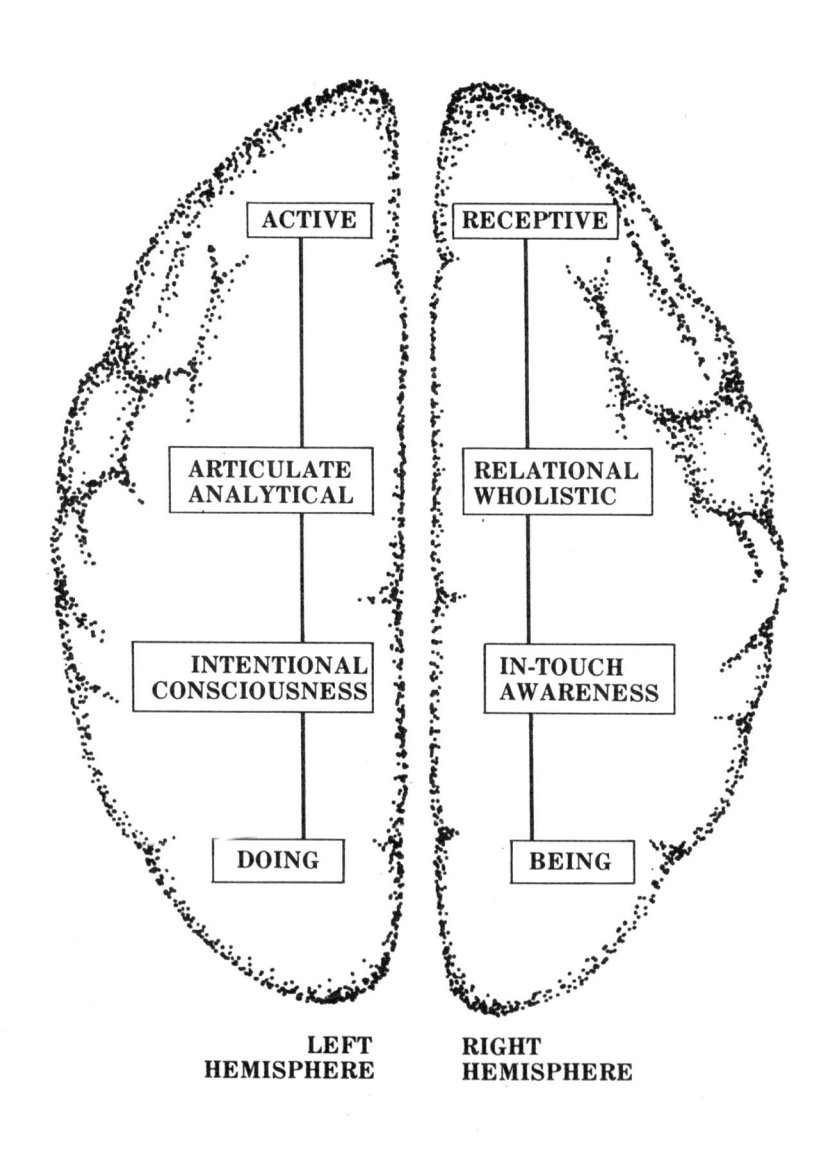

ACTIVE	RECEPTIVE
ARTICULATE ANALYTICAL	RELATIONAL WHOLISTIC
INTENTIONAL CONSCIOUSNESS	IN-TOUCH AWARENESS
DOING	BEING
LEFT HEMISPHERE	**RIGHT HEMISPHERE**

provided us with an analogical map to sharpen our search for wholeness of soul and oneness with God.

In our own time we have seen variations on the theme of fractured faith, or what can be called "split-brain religion." For most of the century the Protestant church (and in recent years the Catholic as well) has been burdened with a split-brain religion of ignorant warmth or arrogant coolness. In earlier years fundamentalists and liberals fought. In recent years activists and pietists have clashed.

At best, uncritical warmth emphasizes the inner life of faith and a sharing witness. At worst, it spawns fanaticism. Similarly, critical coolness at best employs reason in the quest of Christian truth and its contribution to culture. At worst, critical coolness aborts vitality.

When the active and receptive functions are severed, we act in fractured and estranging ways. When these functions complement each other, such wholeness makes for oneness. This, then, is our reflection on pious skepticism.

A Post-Critical Faith

We have grappled with the knotty problems of theology and history, with Paul and the nascent church, with Scripture and the Trinity. And in the end we are brought back to the saying of Jesus: "In my Father's house are many rooms."

Paul was both a Hellenized and a Pharisaic Jew. Yet he could not keep these aspects of his religious identity compartmentalized. He found an integration in Christ, a wholeness (*shalom*) that not only knit the parts together, but transcended them, making him a "new creation." There were indeed "many rooms" in Paul's religious experience, but one house.

While Paul's experience supplied a model for understanding faith in the early church, we have used the human brain

SUMMARY OF PART I

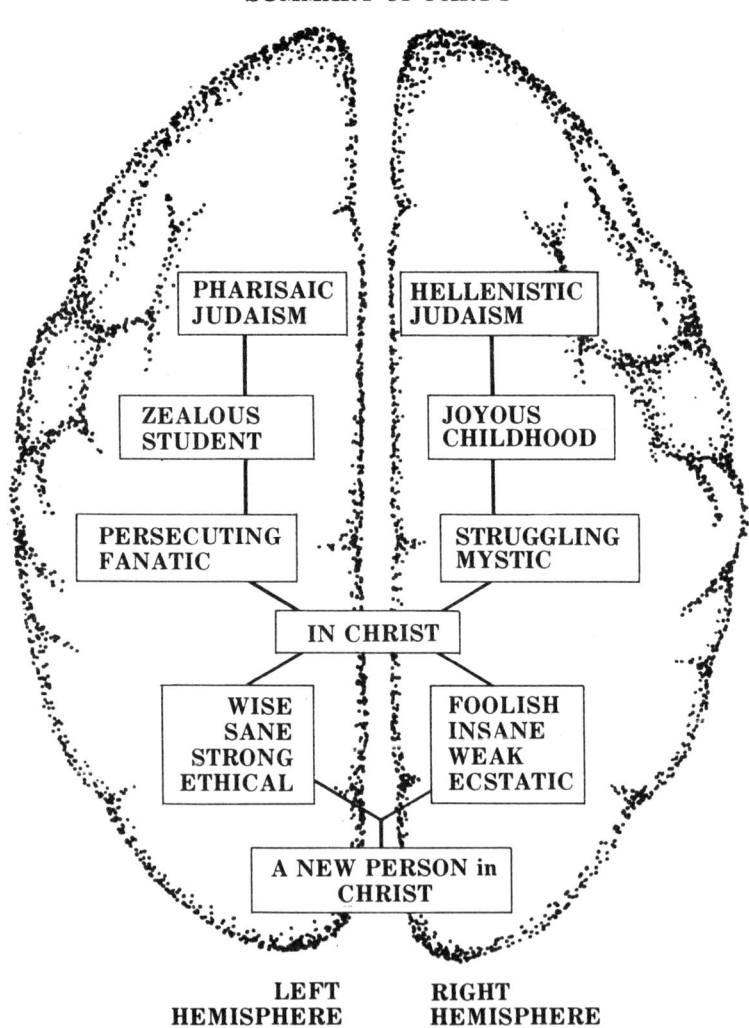

- PHARISAIC JUDAISM
  - ZEALOUS STUDENT
  - PERSECUTING FANATIC

- HELLENISTIC JUDAISM
  - JOYOUS CHILDHOOD
  - STRUGGLING MYSTIC

IN CHRIST

- WISE SANE STRONG ETHICAL
- FOOLISH INSANE WEAK ECSTATIC

A NEW PERSON in CHRIST

LEFT HEMISPHERE   RIGHT HEMISPHERE

SUMMARY OF PART II

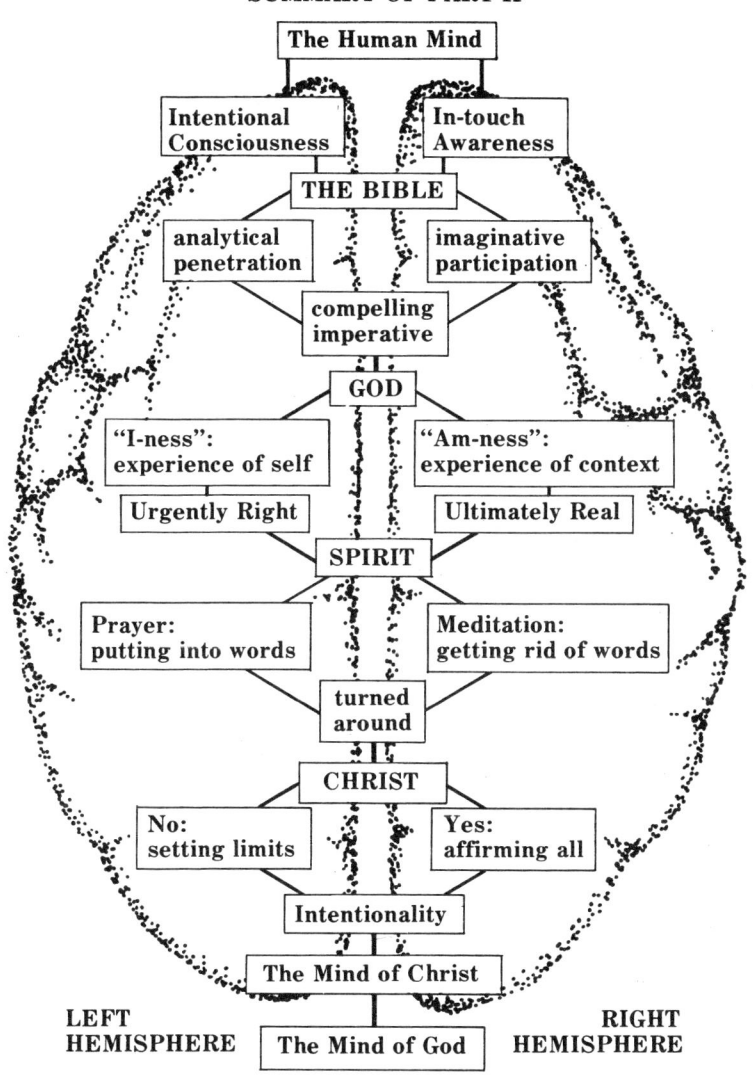

The Human Mind

- Intentional Consciousness
- In-touch Awareness

THE BIBLE

- analytical penetration
- imaginative participation
- compelling imperative

GOD

- "I-ness": experience of self
- "Am-ness": experience of context
- Urgently Right
- Ultimately Real

SPIRIT

- Prayer: putting into words
- Meditation: getting rid of words
- turned around

CHRIST

- No: setting limits
- Yes: affirming all
- Intentionality

The Mind of Christ

The Mind of God

LEFT HEMISPHERE   RIGHT HEMISPHERE

as our model for the contemporary situation. There are two dimensions to our understanding of the Bible, God, prayer, and Christ. The physical dimension has no more (and no less) significance than the psychic dimension. Though distinguishable, the dimensions are inseparable. Each issue connects with the others, requiring them for its completeness.

Our biblical and theological reflections suggested to us that the religious mind is one that has the unique capacity, by virtue of being in Christ, of transcending uncritical warmth and critical coolness. In Christ, piety and skepticism are bypassed as competing claims. We regard that as post-critical faith. In short, the religious mind is the mind of Christ, the integrating mind that overcomes the divine-human separation, that heals a fractured faith, that makes a whole of the parts, that bridges the troubled waters of being and doing. As we began with Paul, so we end with the apostle's version of one of our earliest Christological hymns:

> So if there is any encouragement in Christ, any incentive of love, any participation in the Spirit, any affection and sympathy, complete my joy by being of the same mind, having the same love, being in full accord and of one mind . . . which you have in Christ Jesus. (Philippians 2:1-2, 5)